"Fascinating. In *All Physicians Lead*, Dr. Leon Moores refutes the concept that the surgeon operating on you is simply a highly skilled technician. The West Point graduate and paratrooper-turned-medical-doctor argues persuasively that physicians must be effective leaders who shape our healthcare experience on almost every level, and that our institutions must reflect this requirement. More than a leadership handbook, it is an invaluable roadmap."

STAN MCCHRYSTAL, CEO and Chairman,
The McChrystal Group; Best-selling Author, *Team of Teams: New Rules of Engagement in a Complex World*

"*All Physicians Lead* is a must read for every medical student, young and mid-career physician, and medical educator. It is a reference for self-improvement, advanced curriculum development and ensuring physicians are prepared for the future to lead in increasingly complex times. Dr. Moores draws on his lifelong experience as a military officer and physician leader to define the essentials of physician leadership development that is important in driving positive change in healthcare. Dr. Moores shows how great physicians lead with vision and purpose, helping organizations pivot and remain competitive and relevant to the future. *All Physicians Lead* will be a trusted reference which readers will return to often."

JONATHAN WOODSON, MD, MSS, FACS

"A refreshingly practical and well-written book with the powerful ideas that all physicians are leaders, that leadership can be taught, and that better physician leadership produces better patient outcomes.

All Physicians Lead should be incorporated into every medical curriculum. Dr. Moores' insightful work reflects the synthesis of his impactful careers as a physician and as a military leader in this must-read book."

JAMES K. STOLLER, MD, MS,
Professor and Chairman, Education Institute at Cleveland Clinic;
Author, *Better Humans, Better Performance*

"In *All Physicians Lead*, Dr. Leon Moores delivers a revelation I wish I had encountered on my very first day of medical school. With captivating insights drawn from his military and medical backgrounds, Dr. Moores masterfully portrays every physician as a leader, regardless of their formal role. *All Physicians Lead* is a catalyst for personal and professional growth that leaves a mark on our medical practice and the lives we touch."

J. STEPHEN JONES, MD, FACS,
President and CEO, Inova Health System

"I urge you to read *All Physicians Lead* and allow its timeless wisdom and eminent practicality to seep into your mindset. Leon Moores writes with the voice of an authentic and accomplished practitioner. The most compelling aspect of this seminal work is not simply that Leon can articulate these principles, it is that he lives these principles. It is said the measure of integrity is how one acts in adversity, and I can assure you Leon Moores has faced every adverse situation imaginable and led himself and others through those moments with dignity, grace, and resolve. *All Physicians Lead* is not the latest output from think-tank academics or once-removed consultants, it is the accounting of indelible truths from one who honored them by living them."

DANIEL J. PORTER, Executive Coach; Best-selling Author

"Physician leaders are needed around the world more than ever. *All Physicians Lead* shows every physician how to be a better leader every day and is a must read for them and for the health systems that employ them."

AMANDA GOODALL, Professor of Leadership,

Bayes Business School London;

Author, *Credible: The Power of Expert Leaders*

"This book is a must-read for any physician looking to elevate how they show up as a leader. Dr. Moores offers a timely and practical guide for navigating a new vision for leadership, one that is wholehearted, empathetic, and inclusive. The health care industry has no shortage of challenges and opportunities, and a new cadre of physician leaders is critical to the transformation."

RENEE DESILVA,

CEO, The Health Management Academy

"Dr. Moores is to be congratulated on a unique concept of physician leadership. It is brilliant because it is simple, logical, and inspirational. As a physician and soldier, you will admire that he has taken the most egalitarian route imaginable towards leadership. Dr. Moores beautifully inspires us with the observation that we all lead with our patients. He demonstrates how each of us can do the same with our organizations and health care system. And, I am convinced that Dr. Moores' concept can be practically extended beyond the physician job description. I cannot think of a more hopeful and practical solution, to the leadership challenges that face us in medicine."

RICHARD G. ELLENBOGEN, MD, FACS,

Professor and Chairman of Neurological Surgery, University of Washington School of Medicine; Theodore S. Roberts Endowed Chair in Neurological Surgery; Chief of Pediatric Neurological Surgery, Seattle Children's Hospital

"Leon Moores has crafted an excellent book on physician leadership that makes an important contribution to healthcare. His major premise is that it is just as important for a physician to influence treatment teams to achieve desired results as it is for a physician to have good clinical skills. He notes that good leadership should be exercised by all physicians regardless of their formal title. *All Physicians Lead* is well written and is as enjoyable to read as it is impactful. It should be a must-read by clinicians committed to improving medical practice and health outcomes."

S. ROBERT HERNANDEZ, DrPH,
Distinguished Service Professor and Director,
Executive Doctoral Program in Healthcare Leadership,
University of Alabama at Birmingham

"All physicians are leaders, right? After all, they make decisions directing others—staff, patients, payers, and the like—to do various activities. So what's the problem? As Dr. Leon Moores describes in his book, *All Physicians Lead*, the premise is correct, but, while physicians may be leaders, many do not realize it and even fewer are trained in it. Dr. Moores convincingly argues that making leadership training an integral part of medical education will result in better decisions, more effective teams, and ultimately higher quality patient care!"

RONALD R. BLANCK, DO, MACP,
Former lieutenant general,
US Army; Former Army Surgeon General

"Leon Moores' book, *All Physicians Lead*, is an excellent reference for leadership education for physicians. Making the points that *all* physicians are leaders, leadership is a learned skill, improving physicians' leadership skills makes healthcare function more robustly and efficiently, and perhaps most importantly, the chief beneficiary will be the patients, Moores offers leadership education in a very practical and straightforward way. In today's world of rapidly changing healthcare delivery physicians must recognize their leadership role and improve these skills. Given the legislative and judicial challenges to the principles of evidenced base care and the challenges to the sanctity of the physician/patient relationship, physicians must provide leadership to our communities. Physicians must accept their personal social responsibility in leading in these issues of importance."

JOHN STUDDARD, MD, FCCP

"Leon Moores' unique combination of leadership training and experience provides him with the ability to clearly communicate a proven path for physician leadership development at all organizational levels. His new book is concise and easy to follow, using examples and vignettes to convey his message. A must read for all physicians on their journey to becoming tomorrow's healthcare leaders."

NANCY BORKOWSKI, DBA, CPA, FACHE, FHFMA,
Distinguished professor, University of Alabama at Birmingham

"In *All Physicians Lead*, our colleague Leon Moores has highlighted an opportunity that is so crucial for todays physicians. In convincing language, Leon shows how every physician leads every day and how recognizing and reflecting on that can improve patient health. His passion for this subject and his personal experience combine to give us a valuable resource for these key issues. I trust in him and all he has to offer with education in physician leadership, and I wholeheartedly commend his work to you."

DOREEN J. ADDRIZZO-HARRIS, MD, FCCP
Professor of Medicine, Associate Director,
Clinical and Academic Affairs, NYU Grossman School of Medicine;
2023 President, American College of Chest Physicians (CHEST)

All Physicians
Lead

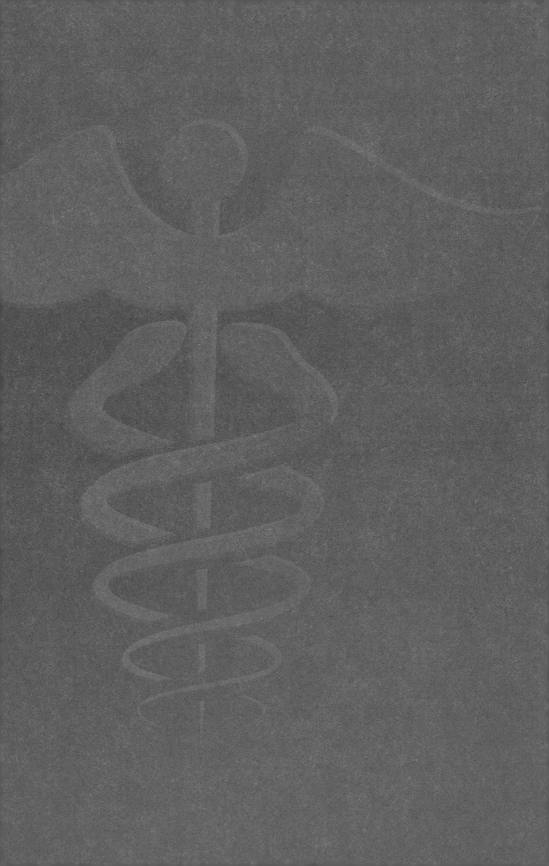

All Physicians
Lead

Redefining
Physician Leadership
for Better Patient Outcomes

LEON E. MOORES, MD, DSc, FACS

Forbes | Books

Published by Forbes Books, Charleston, South Carolina.
Member of Advantage Media.

Forbes Books is a registered trademark, and the Forbes Books colophon is a trademark of Forbes Media, LLC.

Printed in the United States of America.

10 9 8 7 6 5 4 3 2 1

ISBN: 979-8-88750-164-2 (Hardcover)
ISBN: 979-8-88750-165-9 (eBook)

Library of Congress Control Number: 2023915742

Cover design by Analisa Smith.
Layout design by Lance Buckley.

This custom publication is intended to provide accurate information and the opinions of the author in regard to the subject matter covered. It is sold with the understanding that the publisher, Forbes Books, is not engaged in rendering legal, financial, or professional services of any kind. If legal advice or other expert assistance is required, the reader is advised to seek the services of a competent professional.

Since 1917, Forbes has remained steadfast in its mission to serve as the defining voice of entrepreneurial capitalism. Forbes Books, launched in 2016 through a partnership with Advantage Media, furthers that aim by helping business and thought leaders bring their stories, passion, and knowledge to the forefront in custom books. Opinions expressed by Forbes Books authors are their own. To be considered for publication, please visit **books.Forbes.com**.

I humbly dedicate this book to all my pediatric patients and families whose strength, grace, and trust under unfathomable pressures have taught me so much about compassionate leadership. Making it all better for you is what this book is about.

CONTENTS

Let's Change Our Thinking About Physician Leadership

All physicians are leaders. That may not sound like a profound statement, but it really is. And it has vast implications for our healthcare industry. *All* physicians lead, not just those with designated leadership titles, such as Department Chief, Chief Medical Officer, or CEO. Leadership is foundational to the role of doctor. Fortunately, leadership is a learned skill. Improving physicians' leadership skills results in better healthcare. When everyone involved in medicine, particularly physicians themselves, comes to embrace this idea, the entire healthcare system will reap the benefits—nurses, technicians, administrators, finance departments, HR professionals, and doctors themselves. But the chief beneficiary will be patients.

Yes, patients. *Better patient outcomes* are always our goal. And improved physician leadership leads to better teamwork, higher morale, and improved decision-making at every level of the healthcare delivery system. This leads to higher-quality medical treatment, which leads in turn to better health outcomes—for patients.

This simple but powerful idea is the premise of this book: better physician leadership leads to better patient health. But this idea has not yet been institutionally embraced by the medical community. I hope this book plays some small part in changing that. *All Physicians Lead* is more than a book title; it is the foundational concept to drive important changes in medical education and training.

A Bit of Background

How did I come upon this notion that all physicians are leaders and should consciously and deliberately hone their leadership skills? And where do I get the "credentials" to talk about physician leadership? It started at an institution that focuses on leadership development, the United States Military Academy at West Point.

I was fortunate enough, as a young man, to be accepted to West

Point. One of the first things that strikes you upon entering this historic institute is how seriously the US Military takes the concept of leadership and leadership training. When you enroll at West Point, regardless of your background and experience, you start at square one in your leadership development. Every West Point cadet receives a comprehensive four-year program of increasing knowledge, training, and experience in how to lead. By the time you graduate, you've been given four years of continuous leadership education and training, each year built on the foundations of the year before.

And it doesn't stop there. The expectation is that you will continue to grow in your leadership education and development throughout your military career. Specifically, you'll spend about one-third of your career in command, one-third in staff jobs, and one-third in leadership schools. One-third. That's how strong an investment the military makes in training its leaders. For someone with a twenty-year career, that amounts to more than *six total years* invested in learning the next level of leadership.

I chose the Infantry branch upon graduation and I did a tour as a small unit leader in the 82nd Airborne Division. That's when I was able to experience, firsthand, the leadership structure embedded in every level of military life. Leadership training is an ongoing, daily thing for an officer. Your superior officers constantly find "teachable moments" to reinforce your strengths as a leader, as well as to point out the things you could be doing better. Your skills are reviewed, both formally and informally, on a continual basis.

The Army's definition of leadership is "the process of influencing people by providing purpose, direction, and motivation while operating to accomplish the mission and improve the organization." They train you to that definition.

I went straight from active duty in the 82nd Airborne Division to physician training when I was accepted into the Uniformed Services University School of Medicine. The USU SOM is an excellent four-year medical school, accredited like other medical schools. The only distinction is that every student is a commissioned officer in the Army, Navy, Air Force, Public Health Service, or Coast Guard. When students graduate and finish their residency, each has a seven-year obligation to serve in their respective service.

"America's Medical School," as the USU SOM is sometimes called, gave me a terrific medical education, but I noticed one thing right away that surprised me. It was the absence of the structured leadership training I'd become so accustomed to. This seemed a bit odd to me, but I explained it away as, "Well, I guess they're not really training leaders here; they're training physicians." (This has changed dramatically at USU, for the better, see Chapter 9, page 178).

And then I went out into the real world, as a doctor.

I completed a neurosurgery residency and a pediatric neurosurgery fellowship, served as an attending neurosurgeon at Walter Reed and Bethesda Naval Hospital, and was deployed to combat as a neurosurgeon. I saw what physicians do every day. I saw the way we mobilize treatment teams, calm frightened patients, and direct the allocation of resources. I saw the way others look to us to make and execute critical decisions.

An insight dawned: physicians lead *all the time*. It's in the very nature of what we do. We are constantly "influencing people by providing purpose, direction, and motivation, while operating to accomplish the mission (i.e., saving lives)." Almost everything a physician does is a leadership event of some kind, whether in the military or in civilian life.

Physicians are leaders. Period. But we aren't routinely trained as such. To worsen matters, we aren't even explicitly *told* we are leaders unless and until we are promoted to an "official" leadership position. I believe this lack of leadership awareness limits us and, as we will see, blocks much of the reflection and growth that would improve our healthcare system and health outcomes for our patients.

Fortunately for me—owing to the leadership training I had already received—I was given the privilege of serving in increasing levels of "official" leadership within the Army Medical Corps: Chief of Neurosurgery at Walter Reed, Chairman of the Department of Surgery at Walter Reed, Deputy Commander (senior vice president) of the National Naval Medical Center, and Commander (CEO) of the healthcare system centered at Fort Meade, Maryland, which operated fourteen healthcare facilities in four states and had several thousand employees.

As I continued to grow in traditional leadership roles, developing my own leadership skills, I also continued to practice medicine. And I became more and more convinced of the obvious (to me) truth that *all* physicians are leaders, though we rarely train them as such. Consequently, we end up with hit-or-miss results—*some* physicians who carefully develop their leadership skills, others who don't; *some* who are well trained in leadership, some who are partially trained, some who are hardly trained at all. A random assortment of skill levels, a random assortment of functionality.

We could do better than that, I believed. Our patients deserve it. Many studies show that unwarranted variation in care results in poorer health outcomes, and this book will connect the dots between physician leadership and patient outcomes.

Doing Something About It

I decided to try to do something about the issue. When I attained Colonel rank, I went to see a man I had come to know, Major General Richard "Tom" Thomas, the two-star general in charge of the Army Medical Corps. He oversaw all 4,200 physicians in the Army.

I laid out my agenda to him in San Antonio, Texas, over cigars (and maybe a margarita): "I believe all physicians are leaders and should be educated and trained that way. I've been working on this idea for years, and I'd like to put together a program for physician leadership in the Army."

He gave the project his stamp of approval. Over the course of the next year and a half, forty-two leader-contributors and two dozen very experienced senior advisors came together to hash out ideas and ultimately create "All Physicians Lead," a 2013 document that became the Army's core template for physician leadership development and training. [1]

The paper made the case that a cultural change was needed, one in which the Army should begin to view and train physicians as the leaders they are. It then proposed several LOEs (lines of effort) creating a comprehensive, "lifelong" learning environment, in which physician leadership is developed throughout a military doctor's career.

This Book

My hope is that this book will, in some modest way, spur the same kind of change within the nonmilitary medical community. I hope to convince *you* that physicians are leaders, and as such, should be *trained in leadership as a core competency* from the start of medical school. This training should continue throughout their residencies and their entire careers. When physicians become better leaders, the healthcare system works better for everyone—and most notably, for patients.

For whom is this book written? Primarily, it is for doctors themselves. If you are a physician, my goal is to help you start viewing yourself as a leader. When you make that mental shift, something profound happens. You begin to see the connection between your leadership skills and the outcomes you are seeking—high-performance teamwork, lower-stress work environments, and better patient care. You begin to realize that *you* are a crucial vehicle of transformation at every position you hold, at every level of your career.

---

1   Moores, L. E., & Callahan, C. (2013). All physicians lead. The US Army Medical Corps Leadership Development Program.

Sections I and II of the book, therefore, are aimed primarily at physicians themselves. Each chapter starts with a short character vignette, based on real-life events, and then explores an important aspect of leadership development for physicians.

This book is also for anyone involved in the education, training, or employment of physicians—medical school deans, residency and fellowship program directors, hospital administrators, healthcare executives. Section III explores the LOEs (lines of effort) that can be undertaken to develop physician leadership as a core competency from day one of a physician's career. It then looks at specific ways leadership skills can be developed in medical schools, in residencies, in hospitals and healthcare systems, and by physicians' organizations.

These lessons, by the way, apply to any profession where practitioners spend years or even decades perfecting their craft and are then promoted to positions of authority within the organization. I write about physicians because that's the world I know from personal experience, but the principles apply equally well to engineers, attorneys, IT professionals, and many others. This book is for you as well.

Back to healthcare: keep in mind we are talking about changing a culture here. So, this book is for *anyone* involved in or interested in healthcare, not just doctors and administrators. As I hope to show you, developing physicians' leadership qualities can have positive ripple effects across the entire healthcare industry. And the most important effect is improved outcomes for our patients.

Imagine, if you will, a healthcare world in which all physicians show up on the ward, in the ER, or in the lab, skilled in the leadership essentials of sincere caring, excellent communication, consistency of message and actions, professionalism, conflict resolution, and mobilizing high-performing teams.

With your permission, allow me to *lead* you onward…

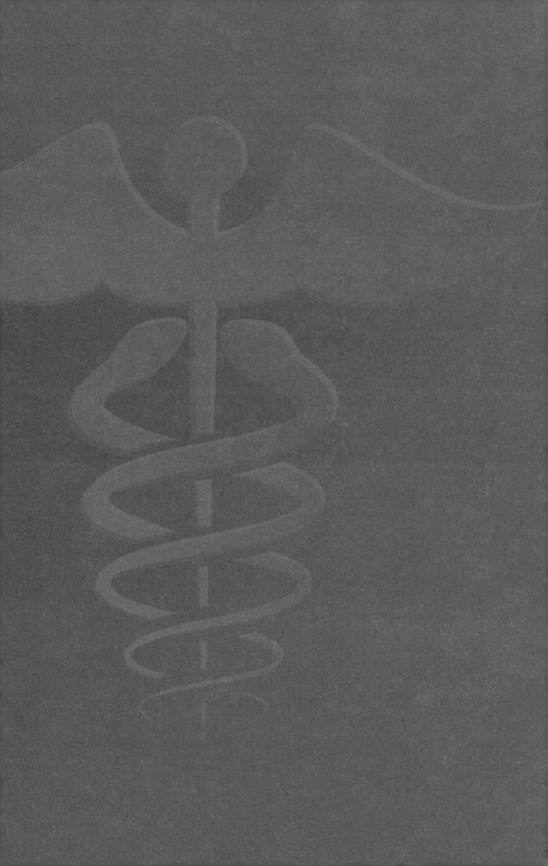

SECTION I

The Value of
Physician Leadership

(Why It Matters)

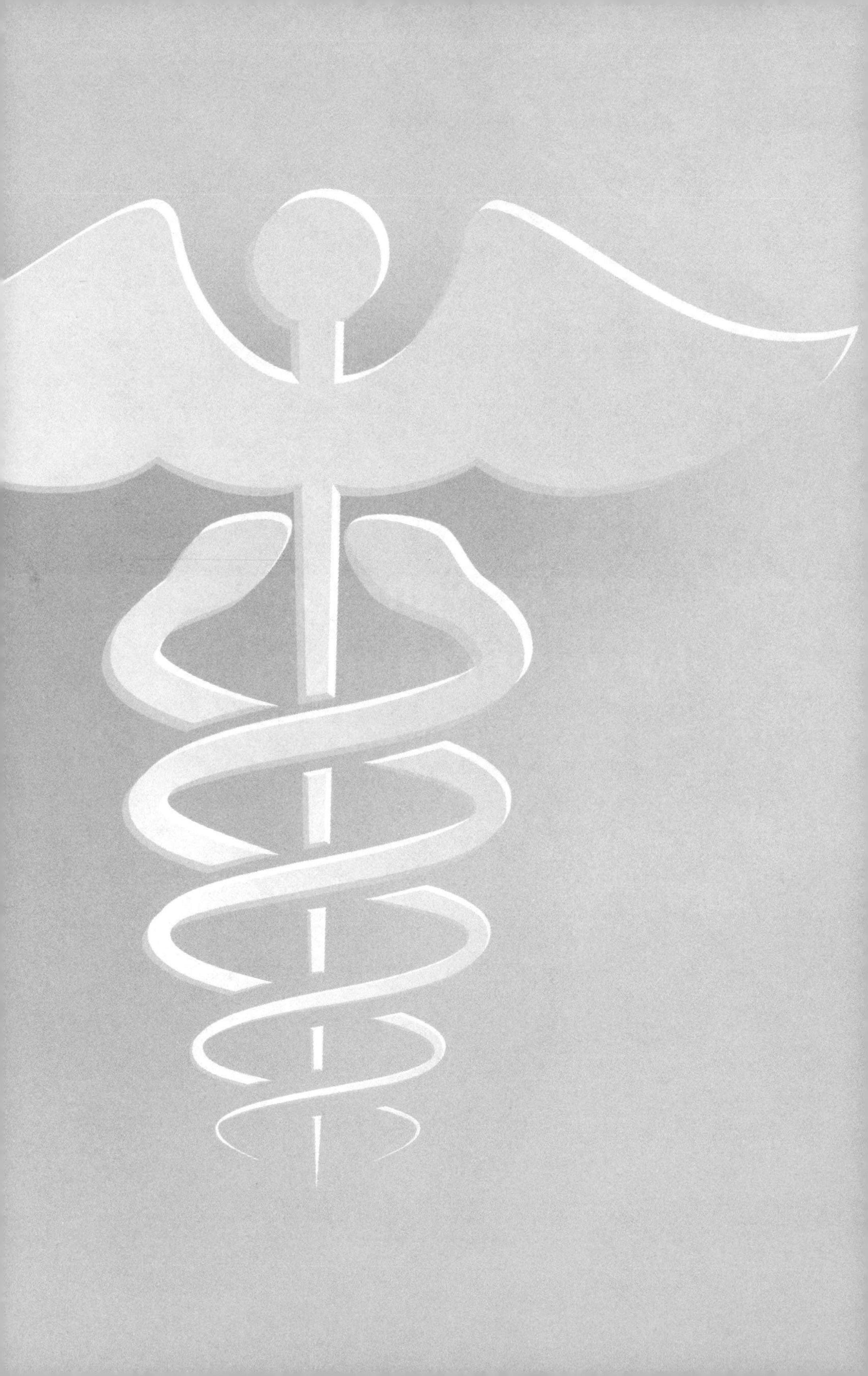

CHAPTER 1

Redefining Physician Leadership

The one quality that can be developed by studious reflection and practice is… leadership.

- DWIGHT D. EISENHOWER

Leadership Scenario 1

After a mishap in the operating room, an attending surgeon slams down his instruments and barks at the OR staff:

"Well done, idiots. This patient will probably die, or at least get a serious infection, because you people can't do your G*******d jobs!"[2]

Leadership Scenario 2

An attending surgeon addresses his OR staff after a sixteen-month-old patient has a cardiac arrest from uncontrollable hemorrhage and dies on the table:

"Quiet, please. I just want to take a moment before you leave to thank each of you for your heroic efforts here today. Things didn't end the way any of us wanted, but no one should leave this room feeling anything but proud of what we did here. This case will be reviewed, certainly, but given what we know today, we did everything we possibly could. You will grieve, as I will, but there should be no shame. None whatsoever. You did excellent work here, and that's the only thing any of us can control. I'm proud to work with you."

Leadership Defined

I google the term "physician leadership," and I get 183,000,000 hits in 0.45 seconds. There are seemingly endless numbers of courses and programs devoted to developing physician leadership. Similarly, if you

---

2   All the leadership scenarios presented in this book are based on actual scenes I have witnessed.

do a book search on Amazon under "physician leadership," you'll be shown dozens of titles. There's no shortage of attention to the topic out there.

Almost uniformly, however, the books and courses approach the topic from a similar angle. That is, physician leadership is something that occurs when physicians reach a point in their career where they are ready to ascend above their everyday role as doctor and lead a department or join the C-suite of an organization. Good physician leadership is seen (rightly) as a vital force for transforming healthcare, but it is almost always viewed from the same perspective: physician leaders are those mid- to late-career doctors who graduate to positions such as clinic chief, department head, or CMO.

Try looking up "leadership" without the "physician" qualifier. You'll find countless definitions of the word, but almost all of them contain some version of this idea: leadership involves an attempt to influence the behavior of others to achieve a desired outcome. With that in mind, allow me to propose a general definition of leadership we can all perhaps accept:

> Leadership is the process of using learned attitudes, skills, and knowledge to influence others' thoughts and behavior to achieve desired results.

We can compress this even more:

> Leadership is influencing thought and behavior to achieve desired results.

Can we agree on this definition? If so, then it's easy to see that leadership isn't something physicians *aspire to* or *work toward* as a "someday" career goal. Leadership is something physicians do every day. We influence thought and behavior to achieve desired results.

Whether we are persuading a patient to stop smoking, a lab to return speedy results, an insurance company to cover a procedure, or a surgical team to understand what needs to be done in the OR today, physicians lead. Leadership is baked into our job.

And the truth is, people already look to physicians as leaders. They expect us to make critical decisions, inspire treatment teams, influence patients' behaviors, present complex concepts in relatable ways, rally patients' families around medical decisions, communicate honestly and empathetically, and be exemplars of professional conduct (and even, yes, of human virtue).

Few roles in society carry as many built-in leadership expectations as that of physician.

However, the current accepted connotation of "physician leader" is overly limiting and refers to doctors in named, obvious positions of authority within the medical hierarchy. I want to convince you to change the conversation and stop viewing physician leadership only through the lens of organizational structures. Let's recognize that all physicians are leaders *now*, not just some doctors later in their careers. Our role requires us to *influence others' thought and behavior to achieve desired results* every day. And those desired results couldn't be more vital: the survival and improved health of our patients.

All physicians lead. Not just Department Chairs, Chief Medical Officers, and hospital CEOs.

The Minute You Put on That Long White Coat

If you are a physician, then from the moment you put on the long white coat on your first day you are engaged in a series of leadership events. You are *influencing thought and behavior to achieve desired results*.

You lead patients

Almost every encounter with a patient is a leadership event. For example, when you sit down with a patient to develop a treatment plan, you're typically trying to convince them to make a change in their life. The desired result may be for them to lose weight, stop smoking, start a new medication, have surgery, or change an unhealthy living environment. In short, you're trying to influence them to do something they weren't doing before and probably don't want to do now.

Dwight Eisenhower, the former US president and military leader quoted at the beginning of this chapter, issued another famous quote: "Leadership is the art of getting someone else to do something you want done, because he wants to do it." That's a pretty good summation of patient relations. Influencing patients successfully requires skills that are fundamental to leaders in all disciplines.

You lead healthcare teams

Every day, you lead treatment teams, whether that's one assistant, a team of five in the OR, the hospital team assigned to your patients, or a whole clinic staff. The "desired results" you're aiming for can change on a daily, hourly, and moment-by-moment basis. For example, you might be facing a logjam in the clinic where patients aren't moving through as quickly as they should, and you're behind schedule. You need to fix it. That's a leadership event. You have a choice as to how to play it. You can vent your frustrations on everyone, shouting, "Come on, people, we need to get things moving!" Or you can use higher-level leadership skills—pull the team together and say, "Okay, we're running behind and patients are getting frustrated. Let's hear everyone's suggestions on how we can fix this." Either way, you're *influencing team members to achieve a desired result.* Sound familiar?

Such leadership situations for physicians—and choices you make in how to handle them—present themselves many times per day.

You lead patients' family members

You're also in a leadership position with patients' families. Here, the desired result might not be to spur a specific action but rather to bring the family to a higher level of understanding. You want them to know what treatments you're planning with their family member, and why. And you want them to know that you care and will do your very best. My experience in pediatric neurosurgery reminds me every day how important this skill can be. You might be asking parents to put their child at risk, via surgery, so you want them to be crystal clear on why you are doing it. You want to listen to all their concerns and mirror those concerns back to them. You want to demonstrate that you care about them and their child. You want them to become as comfortable with this decision as they possibly can be. This is certainly a leadership event of the highest order. It requires fielding difficult questions, giving clear answers, reading people's emotions, listening empathetically, and presenting intricate treatment options with clarity and wisdom.

You lead medical students, residents, and fellows

Part of our training and careers as physicians is to help train other physicians. In this case, the desired result is that they become good doctors. This presents a complex leadership challenge. First, we have to be *aware that we are teaching leadership skills* in addition to clinical skills. Even if we don't recognize we are leading, our leadership behaviors are observed and evaluated by the next generation of doctors. It stands to reason we should reflect on this and recognize we are setting an example for physician leadership—good or bad—every day. Second, we should have a firm grasp on the specific leadership skills we are trying to teach (which we'll talk about in the next chapter). Third, beyond observing residents' technical skills and clinical judgment, we have a great opportunity to pay attention to how they're interacting with the other team members, patients, and families, and coach them on how to do that better. This includes rewarding and complimenting them when they do well as leaders. Fourth, we must constantly *model* all the behaviors we're teaching and coaching. And all of this within a highly stressful environment.

Are you convinced yet that leadership is integral to the everyday life of a physician?

Leadership Is a Core Competency

Leadership is more than a buzzword in business books and seminars. It is a *must* for physicians. *Leadership is influencing thought and behavior to achieve desired results.* As such, it is every bit as important as clinical knowledge and technical skills. It is a core competency.

Competency-based, or outcome-based, education is here to stay. The idea is that, rather than simply requiring a physician to log the requisite number of hours and attain the requisite grades, the physician should demonstrate actual competency in several key areas.

Six core competencies have been identified by the Accreditation Council on Graduate Medical Education (ACGME):

1. Interpersonal and Communication Skills

2. Professionalism

3. Systems-Based Practice

4. Practice-Based Learning and Improvement

5. Medical Knowledge

6. Patient Care

This is a telling and intriguing list. If you look at the six competencies, all of them sit nicely within a mental model of leadership. The first four are obviously tied to leadership. All successful leaders (1) communicate well and relate effectively with others; (2) exhibit sound ethics and an ability to carry out all their professional duties at a high level; (3) understand that all individual practices are part of a larger system and demonstrate an ability to use that larger system to help the patient; and (4) are able to critically evaluate their efforts and continually improve it, based on study, research, and new data.

The last two might not be quite as obvious. (5) Medical knowledge isn't strictly a leadership competency, but of course, nobody will follow a leader who isn't competent in their field. So therefore, knowledge is also essential to leadership. And (6) patient care may sound like it's only about being a good one-on-one caretaker, but it also involves the ability to develop a plan, execute the plan, monitor the plan, and revise the plan. That's Business School 101, and it is absolutely a vital aspect of leadership in any profession.

The ACGME—our designated authority on medical education— has identified these six competencies and tells all doctors-in-training, "You need to know these things." And so, the ACGME is already saying, in a roundabout way, that leadership *is* the most essential aspect of being a physician. But still, these traits haven't been tied together under the *construct* of leadership, and so it isn't necessarily clear why these disparate competencies are important—namely, to influence thought and behavior to achieve desired results.

Bits and pieces of leadership *are* being taught. But because they are presented in a disconnected, piecemeal fashion, many students don't understand why they need to learn them. *How is this helping me take care of patients?* Young doctors may latch onto two or three of these skills as potentially important, but because they aren't looking at the skills holistically, through a leadership lens, they may miss the bigger picture. And because educational institutions aren't seeing the bigger picture either, there are gaps in the courses and curricula they offer. This fragmented approach leads to blind spots.

What I am suggesting in this book is that leadership itself is a core competency. In fact, it is in many ways *the* core competency of being a maximally successful physician. It is the organizing principle under which many other competencies should be grouped. By viewing leadership as *central* to good medical practice—by looking at a physician's skills through the lens of leadership—physicians-in-training can more clearly see the reasons why they must learn all these seemingly disparate skills. And educational programs can fill in the gaps in their training, providing more complete, more longitudinal training in leadership.

The reason for learning leadership as physicians is not abstract or nobly aspirational. Again, it is because we want to *influence thought and behavior to achieve desired results*—with our patients, their families, our team members, our colleagues, and even with the world at large. And the ultimate result we're aiming for is improved health outcomes.

When I've served in executive roles in medicine, I've often taped a large sheet of butcher paper to the back of my office door. It is blank except for a curved arrow that points to the lower right corner, where it reads, "better health outcomes." Whenever anyone entered my office asking for resources or support for a new initiative—whether it be a single staff position or an entire new healthcare facility—I pointed to that chart, handed the person a marker, and said, "Show me how this gets us to better health outcomes." Because that is why all of us went into medicine. That is our prime directive. And if anything we're doing doesn't lead to better health for our patients, then we're focusing on the wrong stuff.

The reason leadership needs to be treated as a core competency is that it will improve health outcomes.

Symptoms of Deficient Leadership Training

Because we don't view leadership as a core competency and train to that competency, the symptoms are felt throughout the healthcare system. I point to these examples not because they are rampant—I don't want to give the impression that this is a typical day in our hospitals and clinics. That said, I am confident that everyone who works in healthcare has witnessed all of these at some point.

Disruptive physician behavior

One of the more obvious symptoms of deficient leadership training is disruptive physician behavior. This can manifest in several ways. Disruptive behaviors include yelling, bullying, demeaning or insulting team members, threatening, chastising team members in front of patients, slamming doors or objects, abusing people's personal space, touching people in an unwanted way, and even physical aggression.

Less obvious, but also insidious, disruptive behaviors include condescension, ignoring others or giving them the cold shoulder, sarcasm, rudeness, failing to communicate or respond, impatience and eye-rolling, dismissive attitudes, and willful miscommunication.

Disruptive physician behavior is a problem that has long been noted by those who work with physicians, and there is a ground-swell of sentiment within the healthcare establishment to eliminate it. People are sensitive to the inherent power differential between physicians and other healthcare workers and are saying it's not okay for physicians to misuse their status.

There are many causes of disruptive physician behavior. First of all, physicians have significant psychological size and power within the medical hierarchy, both because of the financial impact they represent and their historical status, and may seem almost untouchable. People are loath to criticize physicians, and so poor behavior may go unchecked.

Physicians are usually in a hurry. We need to pack a lot into our day, and so it is easy to fall into the habit of being less than fully communicative with team members. A commanding style of communication often seems most efficient. *You, do this. You, do that. Hurry up, let's go.* Physicians are also under a great deal of stress. There is continual pressure on us to make the right diagnosis, the right treatment decision, the right move in the OR or trauma bay or ICU. Our technical and cognitive skills are often tested to the limit. Many physicians hide that stress because they don't want to be seen as weak. But the stress can bubble up in the form of barking at others or having a short fuse.

It's important to note that when physicians are being disruptive, it's not because we are trying to win an Oscar or get a pay raise, it's because we are trying to take care of patients—*to influence thought and behavior to achieve a desired result.* Time always seems too short, lives hang in the balance, and it's easy to feel there are constant obstacles being thrown in the way, stymieing our attempts to get the job done. In addition, we often have a unique understanding of the gravity of a medical situation. A brusque, sharp-toned manner may be a way to impress urgency upon others.

But if the goal is to achieve desired results sustainably—that is, efficient teamwork and good patient outcomes over time—there are better ways to go about this than snapping at people and barking orders. These are lessons that are taught in every leadership course, but almost always lacking in formal medical education programs at every level.

Low-performance/high-stress teams

Low performance in teams is another symptom of our current failure to teach leadership as a core competency. Sometimes low performance is a direct result of a physician's behavior. An example of this is a "code" event where a patient is dying and a speedy x-ray is needed. The x-ray tech walks in and the physician in charge of the code yells, "Hurry up, we need that X-ray now, now, now!" The nervous tech drops the x-ray cartridge, it chips, and he needs to go get another one, costing valuable time for the patient. Or perhaps a tech is trying to get an IV started. The doctor is snapping at her, and the tech keeps missing the vein because her hands are shaking. Not a recipe for success.

Disruptiveness isn't the only way physicians engender poor performance in teams; they sometimes simply fail to provide active, skilled leadership. When constant high demands are made on team members, without a commensurate level of support, caring, communication, mission-awareness, and appreciation of their work, stress is the result. Numerous studies have shown that continual stress in the workplace leads to disengagement, poor performance, employee errors, mental health issues, and increased turnover.

In general, low-performance teams are marked by decreased alignment with the mission or purpose, poor communications, low accountability and transparency, fear of speaking up, absence of role clarity, lack of positive feedback, and an inability of team members to grasp their importance to the mission. All these conditions, as well as those described above, can be treated with a steady injection of good leadership.

Low morale and high turnover

People want their work to matter, and they want to be valued for their contributions. When employees are subjected to high-stress, low-performance environments over prolonged periods, they become disengaged or burned out. Disengagement leads to higher absenteeism, lower productivity, and lower profitability.[3] Morale suffers. The culture becomes one of "keep your head down, keep your mouth shut, and collect your paycheck."

The inevitable outcome of all this is staff turnover. Employees leave for greener pastures. It is often said that "people join organizations, but they leave bosses." When a supervisor does not provide good leadership, the eventual result is that employees find a better job somewhere else. Inability to retain good staff is a huge problem for organizations, especially in today's employee-empowered job environment. Beyond the financial impact of lost productivity, search costs, and time spent interviewing new candidates, the loss of local knowledge and need to retrain the new team members have a negative impact on team performance.

Poor patient outcomes

The ultimate symptom of poor leadership in medical environments is poorer patient outcomes. Of course, leadership is a complex concept, and it is notoriously difficult to draw a direct line from any set of behaviors to specific health results. (That was part of the research I did for my doctorate in healthcare leadership at UAB—there are so many steps between leader characteristics and measurable outcomes, it can be difficult to prove A is the cause of Z with statistical significance.) Still, it stands to reason that poorly led, low-performing teams have poorer results than their high-performing counterparts. When staff members are highly stressed or disengaged, they are more prone to error. Studies show that disengaged employees commit 60 percent

---

3   Karyln Borysenko, "How Much Are Your Disengaged Employees Costing You?," Forbes, May 2, 2019, https://www.forbes.com/sites/karlynborysenko/2019/05/02/how-much-are-your-disengaged-employees-costing-you/?sh=35a875d43437.

more errors than engaged employees.[4] Errors in a medical environment can lead directly to worse patient outcomes.

Disengaged employees, by definition, *engage* less with their job tasks, which, in a medical setting, means patient care. Patients look to healthcare staff to provide communication, encouragement, compassion, attention, care, competence, and confidence in the chosen treatment modalities. When those elements are lacking, patients suffer.

Why Hasn't Physician Leadership "Caught On"?

Physicians are intelligent, highly educated, hard-working individuals, and we care deeply about saving lives and improving the health of our patients. We have demonstrated a willingness to undergo costly, difficult, long-term training to become good doctors, and we strive constantly to improve our skills. So, why aren't all physicians focused on leadership development as a core competency of our profession?

I would argue the reasons are systemic. If physicians-in-training understood the key role leadership played in their careers, they would embrace it wholeheartedly. But that is not the culture into which we doctors are currently recruited, educated, and trained. As a result, physicians often learn leadership only by chance, observation, and self-study. We pick up bits and pieces of leadership along the way. Or perhaps we are fortunate enough to work with a great physician leader, and we become inspired to emulate that person's strengths. In many cases, we *do* strive to develop our leadership skills; we read books and take courses. But again, it's a piecemeal, self-guided approach, not one born of a consistent, comprehensive system.

---

4   Emma Seppälä and Kim Cameron, "Proof That Positive Work Cultures Are More Productive," Harvard Business Review, December 1, 2015, https://hbr.org/2015/12/proof-that-positive-work-cultures-are-more-productive.

Formal education for physicians does not emphasize leadership. Schools may offer leadership-related courses, but because these are not presented in a cohesive, strongly supported way, the skills they teach are perceived as "soft skills"—not nearly as important for the time-starved medical student to learn as anatomy or microbiology. As a result, many physicians develop a habit, early on, of downplaying the importance of leadership skills.

Physicians are superbly educated to serve in our clinical roles, but we're not grounded in the theory and practice of leadership, which I hope I have shown is an important part of our professional role. We are taught to have good answers, provide accurate guidance, and act with authority. But being *designated* a leader does not confer actual leadership ability. For that, a person must be trained.

When we graduate from medical school we are exposed to further gaps in leadership development. Much of physicians' training and modeling is provided by senior residents who may be getting their first taste of leadership but who did not receive much leadership training themselves. Rare is the doctor who cannot tell stories of bullying and humiliation during their residencies.

There's another issue at play that can color doctors' attitudes toward the term "leadership." In physician culture, we sometimes hold a bit of a jaundiced eye toward doctors who leave or reduce their practices to become identified leaders—executives or managers. After all, the further up the hierarchy one goes, the fewer hours one can spend at patients' bedsides. Many physician-executives eventually reach the point where they're putting in only the minimal clinical hours per month to maintain their credentials as physicians. Other physicians may look at these "leaders" and think, "You're not really a doctor anymore, you're just pretending." There's also some chatter that if you choose to take a nonclinical leadership role, maybe you weren't such a great doctor to begin with. So maybe I, as a practicing doctor, don't need to fully respect you (and if you are wondering, yes, I have run headlong into these perceptions). Chasms can develop between "leadership" and the working doctors they aim to serve.

Those chasms are further widened when a physician leader needs to say things to a practicing physician that they don't want to hear—for instance, that they can't have a piece of equipment they ordered. Medicine is a resource-constrained and complicated environment. When you accept a designated leadership position, you often gain a new perspective on how resource allocation decisions are made, and you realize why doctors can't just snap their fingers and get whatever they want. Hospitals must survive financially, and if they go out of business, no one receives any care. But when you try to communicate this idea back to the physician—the person with whom you perhaps once worked side by side—they may think you've sold out to "carpetland" and forgotten who you are. The end result is that to some degree many physicians are averse to being called "physician leader."

I mention the above points because it's important to understand some of the hidden obstacles we will need to overcome as we strive to evolve the concept of physician leadership.

A Page from the Military

If we are serious about integrating leadership training into physicians' careers, we might look to the military for inspiration and modeling. The armed forces know the importance of leadership and leadership training. And they know how to integrate it into day-to-day work life.

When you enter the ROTC or the military academies as an officer-in-training, you enroll in four years of undergraduate training in which you're constantly learning and developing leadership skills.

You continue to hone those skills throughout your career through formal and informal schooling.

Military officers receive feedback on a regular basis. This is true for doctors as well, but there's one key difference. In medicine, you tend to receive feedback only on your clinical or technical performance. In the military, you not only receive *technical* feedback—"You should have checked your map before crossing the stream"—but you also get regular feedback about your leadership skills. This comes in the form of formal written evaluations and informal, day-to-day communications—"That was great the way you praised Sergeant Ames for setting an example, but you missed a teaching opportunity with Corporal Jones." Leadership is so integral to the fabric of the armed forces that it feels completely natural to both coach and *be* coached on leadership every day. The military constantly focuses on sharpening the leadership skillset so that it is engrained in soldiers' "muscle memory."

Imbedding Leadership in Medical Culture

In short, what the military does extremely well is to create a *culture of leadership*. At any given moment, you are not surprised to have your leadership skills praised or constructively criticized by a superior officer. It doesn't seem as if it's coming out of the blue. It is natural and expected. It is baked into the culture.

I believe medicine would benefit by building a similar culture of leadership, in which physicians are identified as leaders from day one and their leadership skills are constantly sharpened and refined throughout their careers. We currently have aspects of this, but we don't support leadership development on a day-to-day, hour-by-hour, moment-to-moment basis.

A culture of leadership starts by stressing, on the first day of training, that a physician is not just a purveyor of care to patients; a physician is an *influencer of behavior who strives to achieve desired results*. Leading is a relational skill; it is not learned in a vacuum. Nor is it spontaneously acquired when one is given authority status. From the beginning of medical school, we can build a culture that emphasizes teamwork. Physicians are members of healthcare *teams*, not solo operators. To use a theatrical example, they're part of an ensemble cast. They are key performers, no doubt, but they are not in a one-person show.

Leadership should be considered a core competency, and leadership skills training built into the medical school curriculum in a focused and meaningful way. It should then be refined throughout the residency years and throughout the physician's career, through specific trainings and through day-to-day, moment-to-moment interactions. When the latter occurs, not only does the "student" receive helpful feedback on their leadership skills, but the "teacher" refines their own leadership process as well. This creates a virtuous cycle in which leadership improves at every level of an organization.

Leadership training should be built into the everyday activities of a doctor. After an OR procedure or a code event, there should be a review, not only of the clinical decisions and actions taken but also of the leadership skills demonstrated and how they might be improved. At team meetings, leadership skills should be a regular part of the agenda. Team members should be provided a safe way to offer feedback on the leadership they are receiving and to voice their leadership needs.

Instead of treating leadership as a "nice-to-have," secondary skillset, we should view it as primary—on a par with clinical skill development. Physicians-in-training should be taught that their ability to *influence thought and behavior to achieve desired results* is vital to their ability to guide patients and coax high performance from their treatment teams—both of which lead to improved health outcomes.

Medical culture should inspire young physicians to embark on a lifelong course of leadership development. In an ideal world, every physician would strive to get better and better at people-skills as time goes on—just as they do with their clinical skills—knowing they will never be "finished" and that there will always be more sharpening that can be done.

It will take time to change the culture of medicine so that leadership skills are viewed as integral to being a physician. But we can move in that direction.

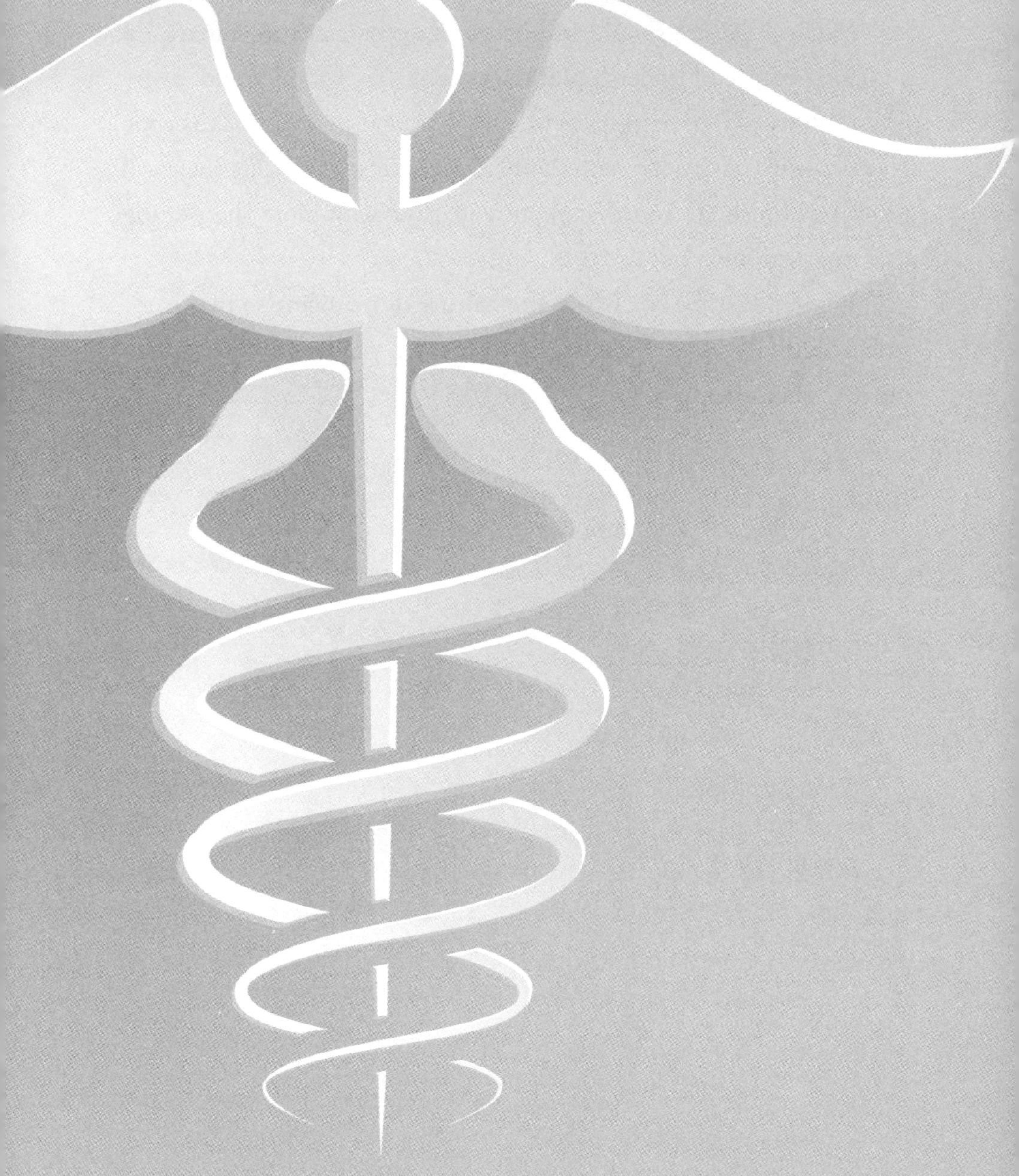

CHAPTER 2

Qualities and Components of Leadership

A leader is one who knows the way,
goes the way, and shows the way.

- JOHN C. MAXWELL

Leadership Scenario

You're the new surgeon at a hospital, and you're shadowing a senior surgeon for the day. During rounds, the senior surgeon examines a patient who has just been admitted with abdominal pain and instructs you to submit an exploratory laparotomy request to the OR scheduler. You know that when surgeries are called in, they are classified and scheduled by urgency level: emergency, urgent, or routine/elective.

Upon examining the patient and reading his records, you learn that his abdominal pain is a chronic problem. The procedure clearly falls into the "routine" category. However, the senior surgeon wants the case done before lunch so she can schedule something else for the afternoon. She intercepts you before you post the procedure and says to you quietly, "Mr. Jones may be a routine case, but I'm going to list him as urgent." She proceeds to do so, and as you're walking away together, she comments with a laugh, "Stick with me—this is how you get things done around here."

We've been talking about the importance of good leadership in hospitals and clinics, and I have been making the case that physicians are leaders by the very nature of their jobs.

But what separates good leadership from bad? What are the traits and behaviors we look for in those whom we designate as leaders? We should be able to agree that the senior surgeon in the above scenario did not exhibit good leadership skills. Although she was certainly attempting to *influence thought and behavior to achieve a desired result*—that is, to train a new surgeon in how to get around "bureaucratic" obstacles—what was the cost? By falsely labeling her case urgent, what potential effect did she have on her fellow surgeons who also have schedules to keep? What effect may she have had on other patients who now need to wait extra hours for *their* surgeries? What message is she sending to the OR team, who likely know this is less than honorable? Is she modeling good professional ethics?

Our definition of leadership as *influencing thought and behavior to achieve desired results* is a good one, and we'll continue to use it, but it certainly doesn't capture all the nuances of leadership. The senior surgeon in the above scenario may (or may not) have been effective in influencing another doctor, but her behavior clearly illustrates that effectiveness is not the sole criterion of good leadership. What are some other criteria, then?

It's not always easy to define good leadership, but, paraphrasing Supreme Court Justice Potter Stewart's famous line, most of us "know it when we see it." When we think back on the great leaders we've worked with, we can't necessarily identify all the qualities that made them great leaders, but we can certainly remember the way they made us *feel*. We likely felt respected and listened to. We probably felt inspired to do our best work. In their presence, we had a sense of mission, a feeling that the work we were doing *mattered*. We knew these leaders would treat us fairly if trouble ever struck. We looked to them as models of what we would like to become. We felt bettered by working with them.

A good leader is more than a checklist of positive attributes. They are often the "sum that is more than its parts." And yet there are many identifiable characteristics that good leaders almost uniformly possess. And for the most part, these are *learnable* traits. As Vince Lombardi put it, "Leaders aren't born, they are made."

Characteristics of a Leader

You'll note this section is not titled "Characteristics of a *Physician* Leader." The qualifier is unnecessary. Although leadership *expresses* itself in specific ways within the healthcare environment, the *principles* of leadership are the same everywhere. There is nothing unique or esoteric about the way we lead as physicians. (So, if you're working on developing your leadership skills, don't limit yourself to books on physician leadership; read great books on leadership, period.)

Let's look at some core leadership traits. The order in which they are presented here isn't significant. They are all important, and they interweave with one another seamlessly and organically. As you will see, it is difficult to talk about any of these traits without talking about others at the same time.

Truthfulness

Truthfulness, and the resultant *credibility*, is a fundamental requirement for leaders. Your team members need to believe you, at a deep and unquestioned level, when you speak. Your word must carry weight. People are listening to you, all the time, not just at those times when you are deliberately addressing them. If they hear you lie or fudge the details in the small things, they may not trust you when it comes to the big things.

We live, unfortunately, in an era where truthfulness, as a virtue, has taken a hit. Political leaders, public figures, and news outlets openly state falsehoods to score short-term victories. They do so flagrantly and without apparent remorse, even though they know their mistruths can easily be exposed. This tactic may work, to some extent, in the short term, but there are long-term costs. One of those is trust.

We cannot afford to let trust deteriorate in our work cultures—especially in medicine, where lives hang in the balance. And so, it falls upon us, as leaders, to create a culture of truthfulness from the top-down. That means *modeling* truthfulness, even when it is personally costly to do so.

Credibility is a hard thing to get back once you have lost it with your team. And healthcare is an extremely unforgiving environment for mistruth. When you're a medical student reporting data about a patient, for example, you can't just make up a sodium level if you didn't actually check it. Blurting out "135" to cover yourself could have deadly consequences. You can't say you examined somebody's appendix when you didn't or tell your team you dosed a medication an hour ago when it was really five hours. Your words must be accurate and verifiable. If people find out you misrepresented medical information, you will have a difficult time retaining trust, not to mention your medical license.

But truthfulness extends beyond accurately reporting data; it includes being honest about your own mistakes, your assessments of your team members, and your reasoning for making decisions. It means not withholding critical information.

Truthfulness can be difficult in the short term, but it has long-term benefits. When you are truthful with your team, they feel respected. They know you're not pandering to them or cushioning them from blows you think they can't handle. When you speak difficult truths in a forthright way, the team feels safe to do the same.

Also, by truthfully acknowledging your own mistakes, you foster an atmosphere where mistakes can be looked at openly and corrected, not stuffed under the rug. You tell your teammates that you place patient care above the need to defend your ego. That builds trust in your intentions as a leader.

Truthfulness about your inner state is also valuable. When you speak honestly about your feelings—within professional limits—

you give your team permission to be more honest about theirs. For example, if you are upset because a patient died unexpectedly, there's nothing wrong with telling your team, "I've had a rough morning, team. I'm good to go, but I might need a little extra energy from all of you today." If your custom is to require only smiling faces from your team, people will feel they need to put up a false front, which can lead to internal tension and emotional distress.

Truthfulness does not mean unvarnished bluntness. Some physicians think it's fine to call out a team member's mistakes or failings, in harsh language, in front of others. But truthfulness should be tempered by compassion and consideration. Praise ought to be given publicly, but "negative" feedback should usually be given privately—unless there is a teachable principle that can benefit everyone. In that case—in any case, really—the feedback should be given respectfully and constructively. Don't hold back what needs to be said, but say it compassionately to avoid defensiveness and pushback.

Truthfulness also does not mean overburdening patients with too much information at once—unless the situation is urgent and dictates that kind of disclosure. When a child comes in with a serious injury and you need to perform a risky procedure to save them, you have no choice but to lay out the stakes for the parents in unvarnished terms. Of course, you'll try to be reassuring as well, but still, they need to understand the risks, and you need to manage expectations. On the other hand, when a child comes in with a brain tumor that's going to take weeks or months to develop, you can deliver the truth in a graduated way. The Hollywood doctor's brusque "This is probably cancer, and it could be fatal" is fortunately rare in real life, for a reason. You won't even have a diagnosis for a week or two. Why burden the parents with the fatal possibilities, until you have all the facts and action must be taken?

Of course, if patients ask specific questions, you should answer them truthfully, but you can still hold back the worst unless they absolutely need to hear it. There's some art to this, and different doctors approach it differently. But we can all find a way to remain truthful without being unfiltered to the point of hurtfulness. Because when we are "too truthful," we can also lose our team's trust. They no longer trust our ability to be sensitive and emotionally intelligent. They dread how we're going to handle situations where tact is required.

Accountability

Closely related to truthfulness is accountability. Accountability, and the resultant integrity, has several aspects. From one angle, it can be regarded as the future tense of truthfulness. When we say we're going to do something, we do it. Our promise is sacred. Our word is our guarantee.

Accountability is the future tense of truthfulness.

Accountability, from another angle, means to not just talk the talk but to walk the walk. When we ask our team to change a behavior, such as to be more communicative or punctual, we embody that behavior ourselves. We don't ask the team to do something we are not willing to do. Rather, we follow Gandhi's advice: "If we could change ourselves, the tendencies in the world would also change."

There is also an element of "the buck stops here" to accountability. Accountable leaders take responsibility for their decisions and accept the consequences without blaming others. They never throw team members under the bus, and they stick up for them when they come under fire from outside forces. When the team fails, they hold *themselves* accountable first. Great leaders live by the credo that when things go well, you give away the credit, but when things go badly, you take the blame.

Accountability in a work culture means that everyone does the job they are assigned, and they do it thoroughly and conscientiously, each taking full responsibility for their actions. This type of culture starts with the leader. The leader makes sure everyone understands the role they are playing and holds everyone accountable for doing their job.

At the risk of annoying many readers, I will cite the New England Patriots—particularly in the Brady–Belichick era—as a great illustration of accountability. Every Patriots player, when interviewed, would unfailingly say that the culture of the team was to do the job they were assigned, with complete attention, no more, no less. Coaches took full responsibility for teaching the players their roles, and players took full responsibility for executing them. When the team won a game, both Brady and Belichick would deflect all the credit to the players. When the team lost, the two leaders would say, "I need to do a better job distributing the ball," "I need to do a better job preparing the team," and so on. The buck stopped at the leaders. For twenty years, the Patriots were arguably the highest performing team in football.

Professionalism

Another vital characteristic of a leader is professionalism. A key part of professionalism is to thoroughly understand your job and the job your team is doing and to be an exemplar of the skills you are expected to possess. This is especially important in medicine. A good leader should be a competent physician with excellent skills and exceptional knowledge. If leaders are less than fully competent, they will not win the respect of the teams they are trying to lead. The physician should be able to teach skills to others, both directly and by example, and should be comfortable being observed.

Professionalism also refers to your everyday behaviors as a leader. The behavior you display will be emulated by team members. This is a major part of building a culture. Junior physicians model their behavior after the type of professionalism they observe in senior doctors. And so, in addition to embodying good medical behavior, physician leaders must exhibit a range of behaviors that "professionals" in all fields exhibit—timeliness, respectfulness, good social skills and boundaries, appropriate dress, attentiveness, good eye contact, and a confident voice. They must also avoid "unprofessional" behavior, such as gossiping, playing favorites, rudeness, oversharing of personal details, and inappropriate jokes or comments, to name a few. I once had a commander who told me "self-deprecating humor is the only kind commanders can afford." That philosophy works with physicians as well, because of the power dynamics we've discussed.

Good communication skills

If leading is *influencing thought and behavior to achieve desired results*, then communication is the main way we accomplish this. As physicians, we can't afford to regard communication skills as secondary to clinical skills. The two go hand in hand.

Communication skill starts with a *willingness* to communicate. Regardless of whether you are a naturally communicative person or not, you must develop the habit of communicating regularly with your team. And you must constantly work on upgrading your communication skills with patients. The better you can communicate with patients, the more effectively you can *influence their thought and behavior toward better health outcomes*. You should be able to communicate with patients of widely different ages and backgrounds. This involves developing a measure of cultural competence (we'll talk about this in Chapter 5). The language you use and the degree of empathy and cultural sensitivity you demonstrate will strongly affect how compliant patients are with therapy. So, every exchange with a patient is a leadership event—you're trying, as Eisenhower suggested, to get them to do something *you* want because *they* want to. And the biggest part of this is communicating in a way your patients understand and buy into.

As physicians, we are naturally caring people. We care about our patients. But if this caring is not *communicated* to patients in an overt fashion, it might not be understood. You can care as much as you want, but if you're facing away from them, typing on a computer throughout your consultation, they may not feel it. And they may be less likely to follow your leadership.

Likewise, the way you talk to your team will influence their willingness to follow you and perform at the top of their game. Good staff communication is not just a matter of being open and personable, it's also a matter of imparting good data. Are you giving people enough information so they fully understand the plan? Have you drawn enough information from *them*? Have you asked for their feedback?

We tend to think that because we can see the whole picture in our heads, others can see it too.

Might there, for example, be a better way to assemble the medical equipment or prep the patient? You won't know unless you ask.

Details can be easily overlooked. The human brain operates under a great many cognitive biases. These are essentially blind spots that lull us into making bad assumptions. One of these is the so-called "curse of knowledge" bias: we tend to assume others have enough background knowledge to understand what we're saying when we speak in shorthand. We also tend to think that because we can see the whole picture in our heads, others can see it too.

Have you explicitly given your team enough of what's in your head that they know what you're thinking? *You* may be able to fill in the unspoken gaps, but can *they*? One way to be sure is to ask your people to repeat back what they heard you say. This should be a routine communication habit in a high-stakes environment.

Service-mindedness

When we think of leadership, many of us think in terms of career advancement: a person works years in a rank-and-file position and then earns a leadership post, which confers a certain amount of power and prestige. This is a limited way of viewing leadership, for a couple of reasons. First, as I have been emphasizing, physicians are leaders from day one; leadership is a foundational part of our job. But second, leadership should have little to do with prestige. Particularly in healthcare, it should be appreciated as a service position. True leaders understand that they serve and care for those whom they lead. A leader's job is to understand how they can bring out the best in their patients and teams and give them what *they* need. "How can I help?" is their mantra.

In my army experience, when soldiers and officers were fed meals in the field, the commander ate last. This was a symbolic gesture—we rarely ran out of food—but it sent the clear message that you take care of your people first. Yes, the mission is critical, but you can't accomplish the mission without your people. In a hospital environment, you may not need to worry about whether your team has literally eaten (although this *can* be a concern on very hectic days), but you want to do everything in your power to ensure your people know they are part of a team and that you have their backs—and that if they make a mistake, the team will recover from it together. Leadership is not about you as the doctor. It's ultimately about the patient and *achieving better patient outcomes*. And everyone on the care team will perform better toward that end if the physician leader is taking care of *them*—physically, educationally, and emotionally.

Empathy and emotional intelligence (EI)

Our general cultural understanding of leadership is changing, for the better, and we now expect leaders to possess a healthy measure of emotional intelligence (EI). A key part of EI is empathy—the ability to read other people and the willingness to consider how they are really doing. If somebody in your team is having a bad day, you should have the empathy to recognize this, as well as the skills to find out what the problem is and to show them you care.

Empathy is not a new idea in healthcare. Most of us were taught as student doctors to be empathetic toward patients. But do we practice empathy toward our *teammates*? Paying attention to the stress they're under can go a long way to help relieve that stress. We should recognize that our teammates bring their entire selves to work. If there are major problems going on at home, how might that be affecting job performance?

COVID-19—especially in the early days when we knew very little about the disease—taught us a great lesson on the need for empathy toward our teammates. People were coming to work and taking care of patients, knowing they themselves might get sick and die—or bring the contagion home to their families. When you walked through a hospital ward in those days, you knew everyone was worried about the same thing. Fear was the elephant in every room and corridor. As physician leaders, it was incumbent on us to go the extra mile to reach out to team members and ask how they were doing, how their families were, or whether they just needed to talk. It was an extremely difficult time, but it was also a time when strong and lasting bonds were built. It's possible to build bonds in noncrisis times by creating a culture of empathy and caring around you.

When it's said that people don't care how much you know until they know how much you care, this is what they are talking about.

Character

"Character" is one of those words leadership books throw around. But it's a hard quality to pin down, and it means something slightly different to everyone you ask. Like "good leadership," it tends to be one of those qualities you know when you see. We tend to think of character as an innate trait—"She's a person of good character." Some people have it, while some people don't. We praise people who possess it, but avoid people who don't.

But if character is an inborn trait, like height or eye color, then there's nothing we can do about it. And I, for one, don't accept that. It lets us off the hook too easily. It has been my observation that every positive human trait is one that can be learned and improved upon.

In a sense, character is a combination of many, or all, of the other characteristics we have talked about so far. After all, if you are truthful, empathetic, accountable, capable, and service oriented, then it would certainly be fair to say that you have good character. And all those component traits are learnable.

There's another way of thinking of character that may be helpful. That is, to use the word as it is used in theater and cinema. Character is a role someone plays. We measure actors' performances by how well they fulfill the expectations of the role they play. When you take on a leadership position, such as physician, you are similarly agreeing to play a role. And that role is someone whom people trust and want to follow, and whom they count on to make good decisions and to support their efforts on the team. Do you act in ways that support that role?

Roles on sports teams are a good example. When you accept the role of quarterback or team captain, or any leadership position, you take on a responsibility to exhibit qualities that make the team better, stronger, and more cohesive. This includes your off-the-field behavior. You are expected to embody the values the team aspires toward. That's part of the role, the job. And when you're *on* the field, your role is to support the team's performance. You can't just yell and scream at people—that won't help the team win. The team needs to trust you.

The trust you build, day in and day out, by being supportive, trustworthy, honest, communicative, and accountable—in other words, by having good "character"—buys you loyalty and high performance from your team. That loyalty kicks in when circumstances, such as a medical emergency, rob you of the "luxury" of being democratic or empathetic. You can then snap your fingers and shout a command, and everybody will follow because you'll have built that trust, through the character you've exhibited every day, when things weren't in crisis.

When we view character through that lens, it's easy to see how it helps *influence thought and behavior to achieve desired outcomes.*

A Leader Provides...

The role of leader is evolving. People now look to leaders to provide not only traditional "supervisory" elements such as guidance, orientation, task assignment, and discipline but also to provide...

Consistency

A sense of consistency is one of the most important environmental factors leaders can provide. People need to believe the same rules apply every day. One of the worst traits a leader can exhibit is unpredictability. If you yell at people for doing something one way, and the next day you yell at them for *not* doing it that way, you paralyze the team. People are unable to behave based on organizational norms, because there aren't any. They need to ask permission for every action, because they don't know whether the answer will be yes or no.

You may recall Maier and Seligman's famous experiments with rats using BF Skinner's operant conditioning box. In the Skinner box, certain behaviors would trigger a food pellet for the rat, and certain behaviors would trigger an electric shock. The rats quickly learned how to behave in a way that earned pellets and avoided shocks. However, in experiments that produced an unavoidable shock, randomly delivered, the rats would make no attempts to escape and would devolve into "learned helplessness." The rat had no idea what to do. Inconsistent leadership leads to a version of this in our teams. In medical school, we would sometimes look at each other, defeatedly, and say, "I'm belly up in the Skinner box," to signify we had no idea what on earth was being asked of us. This state is the antithesis of what good leadership provides.

Psychological safety

A high-performing team is one where everyone is respected and where everyone contributes their ideas and expertise to make processes run more effectively and efficiently. This can be achieved best in a culture where team members' feedback is actively sought and where people feel safe speaking up. *Psychological safety* refers to a work environment in which everyone feels free to speak their minds without fear of reprisal and without concern that they may be breaking a taboo.

Establishing psychological safety in medical environments can be challenging. That's because, as doctors, we wield tremendous psychological size, as I said before. Our title confers a certain standing in society and in the medical community. Patients and healthcare workers tend to give us a great deal of deference and a wide berth. Sometimes the only person who feels free to speak their mind around us is the tough-as-nails, twenty-five-year veteran nurse.

But we want to hear everyone's voices. Everyone in the clinic has a valuable perspective, and they all have thoughts and observations we should know about as decision-makers. But if we're not encouraging them to speak up, they won't. And so, we must offer such encouragement proactively and consistently—because we're fighting against centuries' worth of social conditioning that says, "The doctor knows best, and you shouldn't challenge the doctor."

Fortunately, this situation is changing (and we'll talk shortly about how physicians can help drive that change), but we're still not where we need to be. People still feel intimidated around physicians, and wherever intimidation exists, psychological safety is diminished. So, it's on each of us, as physicians, to ask questions of our teams such as, *Hey, did anyone see anything we could have done better today? What was your impression of this procedure? When things went sideways, how did you feel? What was your response?*

Psychological safety starts with not yelling at or demeaning anyone. But it goes beyond this. And it goes beyond even being neutral and assuming, "If anyone needs to say something to me, they'll say it." Neutrality isn't enough to counteract our power differential and psychological size. Doctors, especially those with graying temples and a few years of practice under their belt, have a gravitas that must be actively overcome. I see this in my own life and work. People have a very difficult time not calling me "Doctor Moores," even after I repeatedly tell them to call me Leon. We doctors have an affirmative duty to almost bend over backward to ensure that both patients and staff people can speak their minds honestly around us. When people keep quiet treatment possibilities and case details may be missed.

Psychological safety applies to patients, not just healthcare teams. It is of utmost importance that patients feel free to be completely honest with their physicians. This is especially difficult for older patients who were raised in an era where doctors weren't supposed to be challenged. That's why I make a habit, at the end of every patient visit, of saying, "Does that make sense to you? Are there any other questions? Is there anything I said that you want to talk about? Are you comfortable with the plan?" I sprinkle questions like these throughout the visit, but I always ask them again at the end. And if I see any sign of discomfort or holding back on the part of the patient, I'll press the issue a bit. "You don't seem completely comfortable. What's on your mind?"

Problem-solving and transparency

In any field, people look to leaders to solve problems. That's part of the job description. But *open and transparent* problem-solving is a skill of true leadership. Anytime a problem arises—and this happens all day long in medicine—you have a choice to either solve it internally, behind closed doors or a closed mouth, or to solve it in real time, in front of people, letting them in on your thinking process. When you talk through a problem, sharing your thoughts, you create teaching and modeling experiences for those around you.

By giving people the benefit of your problem-solving process, they learn that solutions don't magically appear in a doctor's head.

Rather, physicians weigh various options, discounting some and raising others to a higher status to get to a final idea. Transparent, real-time problem-solving helps promote psychological safety; when you work through a solution aloud, you show that you are fallible, just like everyone else. You model open communications. And you create opportunities for team members to chime in with ideas you might be missing.

Cultural modeling

Culture is the lifeblood of any human enterprise. Culture is the mood, the vibe, the living value system of an organization. Employees are always looking for outward signs to help them grasp the work culture. *What defines us? What is appreciated and rewarded here? What is considered taboo? What is our service philosophy?* They especially look to their leaders for signs.

Leaders should be the embodiment of the culture they wish their teams to adopt and their patients and families to experience. You can't preach one thing and live another. You must model the culture you wish to see flourishing around you. For that reason, it's important to work for an organization whose culture you believe in and to take it upon yourself to be an exemplar of that culture. It's also important to lead your team to model behaviors you want the organization to adopt or get better at. We'll talk more about culture later.

Inspiration and a sense of mission

Perhaps the most important "intangible" a leader provides is a sense of mission. People inherently crave purpose. Meaning. They want to believe the work they're doing *matters*. A sense of purpose carries people through difficult days (or months, or even years, as with COVID) and provides an antidote to burnout. A good leader embraces the responsibility to *inspire*.

In medicine, as I said earlier, our purpose couldn't be nobler or more important. We save lives. We extend lives. We improve lives. It's up to you as a physician leader to reinforce this mission on a daily basis, to not let people grow blasé about the work we do.

One way to keep a sense of mission alive is by having a clear sense of what *winning* looks like for your team—happier patients, healthier patients, patients who have survived severe health episodes—and to continually praise and reward team members for daily victories. *That was amazing work, Joan. Look how well this patient is doing because of your efforts.*

It's just as crucial to keep people inspired when things go wrong. For example, when a young patient dies on the operating room table as we saw at the beginning of Chapter 1, you have a choice as to how you respond. You can tear off your scrubs and stomp out of the room, leaving everybody feeling even worse. Or you can take a deep breath, get your emotions under control, and take things *up* a level. Praise everyone for the work they did and for "leaving it all on the field." And if things were not done perfectly, vow to learn from the experience to save even more lives in the future.

Conflict resolution

Managing and resolving conflict in a safe, healthy, and productive way is another critical role leaders provide. I do a lot of teaching and lecturing in this area, and one point I always emphasize is that conflict is not a bad thing. Passionate disagreement is a sign that people are engaged. The opposite scenarios are worrisome—when people feel they need to stifle diverging opinions or when they just stop caring.

Sometimes when we hear the word "conflict," we think of people behaving badly, such as throwing tantrums or insulting one another. That isn't conflict, that's people behaving badly. And that needs to be dealt with quickly and unequivocally. If someone's behavior is negatively impacting the team, you must address it. If, as a leader, you do not, you are effectively condoning it.

But healthy conflict can be used to enhance team communications and improve processes. As a leader, you want to encourage debate and open communication. You want people to feel free to say, "Hey, I disagree. I don't see it that way." Your job is to provide a safe space for people to voice opposing opinions and to make sure disagreement doesn't carry a negative connotation.

If there are interpersonal issues on your team—personalities that don't get along, for example—your job is to facilitate open communication about this. Give all the parties a chance to speak and be heard by the others. Emphasize shared goals and desires, such as excellent patient care, and stress the value of having different types of people on the team. In most cases, when people understand each other better they give each other more leeway and respect. I have even seen many situations where teammates with conflicting personalities become each other's fiercest advocates when the team is "under attack." This type of outcome often results from the positive sense of team identity the leader has created, and the leader's own willingness to fight for the team when it faces adversity.

Positive versus Negative Leadership

In a very general sense, we can talk about leadership in terms of negative leadership and positive leadership. These are sweeping terms, of course, but they are useful for our discussion because they describe near-universally accepted behavioral traits.

Negative leadership refers to a style marked by autocratic rule, beratement, yelling, threats, shaming, micromanagement, and negative consequences used as a first line of discipline (e.g., "Shape up or I'll fire you"). There is an implied adversarial relationship between the leaders and the led, and a general use of fear as a motivating factor.

Negative leadership can also be a style of leadership marked by neglect, inattention, indecisiveness, lack of vision, weak communication, and poor conflict resolution—a failure to lead actively and strongly. Yet another way of viewing negative leadership is that it focuses excessively on correcting errors as opposed to building strengths and competencies. It lacks a guiding vision.

Positive leadership, on the other hand, is characterized by encouragement, vision, respect for each team member, fairness, striving for team improvement, clear and open communications, the rewarding and praising of desired behaviors, and an atmosphere of active learning.

In medicine, a physician's use of negative leadership traits does not necessarily imply that he or she is a negative person. More often, it is a function of lack of awareness and training. Most physicians who fall into negative leadership habits do so for two key reasons:

1. They do not realize they are leaders—or that leadership simply means *influencing thought and behavior to achieve desired outcomes.* The resulting lack of reflection and insight into the impact of those negative leadership behaviors allows them to persist.

2. They do not realize that leadership requires an actual skillset and is not merely a status attained. They confuse authority with leadership. Institutional tolerance and enabling of negative leadership behaviors reinforces the lack of impetus to change.

Again, much of the blame for this mindset rests with our historical lack of recognition that all physicians are leaders and the failure to adequately train them as such, a history this book aims to help remediate.

Fortunately, institutions and healthcare organizations, and their people, are learning that consistency, EI (caring), vision, communication skills, and empathy create better work environments and improved outcomes. The demand signal is there, the option to respond is available. It is our choice.

Positive leadership requires a positive attitude

Leadership doesn't happen in a vacuum. If you want to lead positively, you can't walk around with a resentful, angry, defeated, or "eye-rolling" attitude. You cannot let negative circumstances get the better of you. Negativity is surprisingly common in medicine—not usually toward patients but often toward aspects of the healthcare system. When physicians walk around complaining about the administration, regulations, or (most frequently!) the electronic medical record, that doesn't ultimately help the team. That doesn't give them confidence that they're being supported by the organization from top to bottom. Complaining influences thought and behavior, but in a net-negative way.

As a leader, rather than complaining about "the idiots in carpetland," you have a certain responsibility to get to know the system better and to try to comprehend the reasoning behind the rules and regulations. You need to make a reasonable effort to see the big picture and understand some of the pressures senior executives, strategic planners, compliance officers, and finance departments are under. If you can understand why the system is set up the way it is, you may be able to help your team view some of the irritating rules of the job in a larger context. Though it might seem more satisfying to play the card of "We're the real heroes down here on the floor; the suits upstairs are just a bunch of out-of-touch bureaucrats," this approach may drain people's energy in the long run and make them less likely to seek management positions themselves. To quote the leadership and management guru Paul Bataldan, "All organizations are perfectly designed to give you exactly the results you are getting." If you want to change the organization, and the results, you have to lead.

Of course, many aspects of healthcare *are* overregulated. Healthcare teams *are* forced to spend a lot of time doing non-value-added work. Fighting with insurance companies *is* a pain, as is working with the added requirements of electronic health records. And we should all work to improve these things. But meanwhile, the attitude we should take as leaders is *Yes, we're obligated to do these things, and none of us like them, but let's keep our focus on saving lives anyway.* You don't have to pretend everything is rosy, but you do need to lead effectively *through* the drawbacks and in spite of them.

One of the challenges leaders in all fields face is to lead through changes they didn't direct and that they don't necessarily agree with. In such cases, you can either resist the change or you can take a strong positive leadership position and say, *Okay, it is what it is. How do we make this work better for our patients and teammates?*

We also need to be able to lead, in a positive way, when our best-laid plans go to pieces. We may think we've anticipated every contingency in a medical procedure or in a day at the clinic, but as militaries have known for centuries, "the enemy has a vote." Things can, and do, go sideways fast. No matter what you think is going to happen, it won't happen the way you thought. You need to be able to lead through the unexpected—with a positive attitude that lifts people up instead of burdening them further. A sense of humor often helps.

Leading the change in our role as physicians

I also believe we physicians need to lead through the tectonic change that is happening to our own role in medicine and society. The historic model of doctor as an untouchable authority figure has been disintegrating for some time now (and rightly so, I believe).

The old formula for leading as a physician was, "Position + Credentials + Legal Authority = Compliance." The old formula doesn't work anymore, if it ever really did. Leadership is evolving, and the new role people are demanding for doctors is as team member, communicator, and healthcare collaborator, not as infallible autocrat. Patients have demanded the change, as have hospital systems, nurses, younger doctors, and society at large.

Some of us welcome this change; others perhaps not so much. Traditionalists may view it as a loss of prestige and power. But as with any cultural change, we can respond in two ways. We can dig our heels in and resist the change. Or we can say, *What's the most positive outcome we can create here?* And we can *lead* the change, adding our perspective and energy to it. We can help ensure the change happens in the most positive way possible.

The fact is, we lose no credibility because of this change in our roles; rather, we gain. By being more receptive to input from our patients and coworkers, we're able to make medical decisions that will be more effective. We're able to recruit and retain high-quality staff who now feel more respected, listened to, and fulfilled. And we're able to give patients the sense of empowerment over their own treatment many expect. By being fully on board with the change—by leading it, not following it—we have an opportunity to create higher-performing healthcare teams than ever before. And better patient outcomes.

For the most part, this just means making small adjustments throughout the day and week. Take a couple of minutes with each

54

patient to connect with them on a human level. Take moments with staff too, throughout the day, to solicit their feedback and points of view. Ask if there's anything they need from you. Express gratitude and give praise. Ask folks how they're doing. Be the humanizing element within your office. Again, if you take the time to do this when things are relatively calm, your team will be ready to jump into action under your command when lives hang in the balance. They will perform like a well-oiled machine because they respect you as a leader and want to give their very best for you.

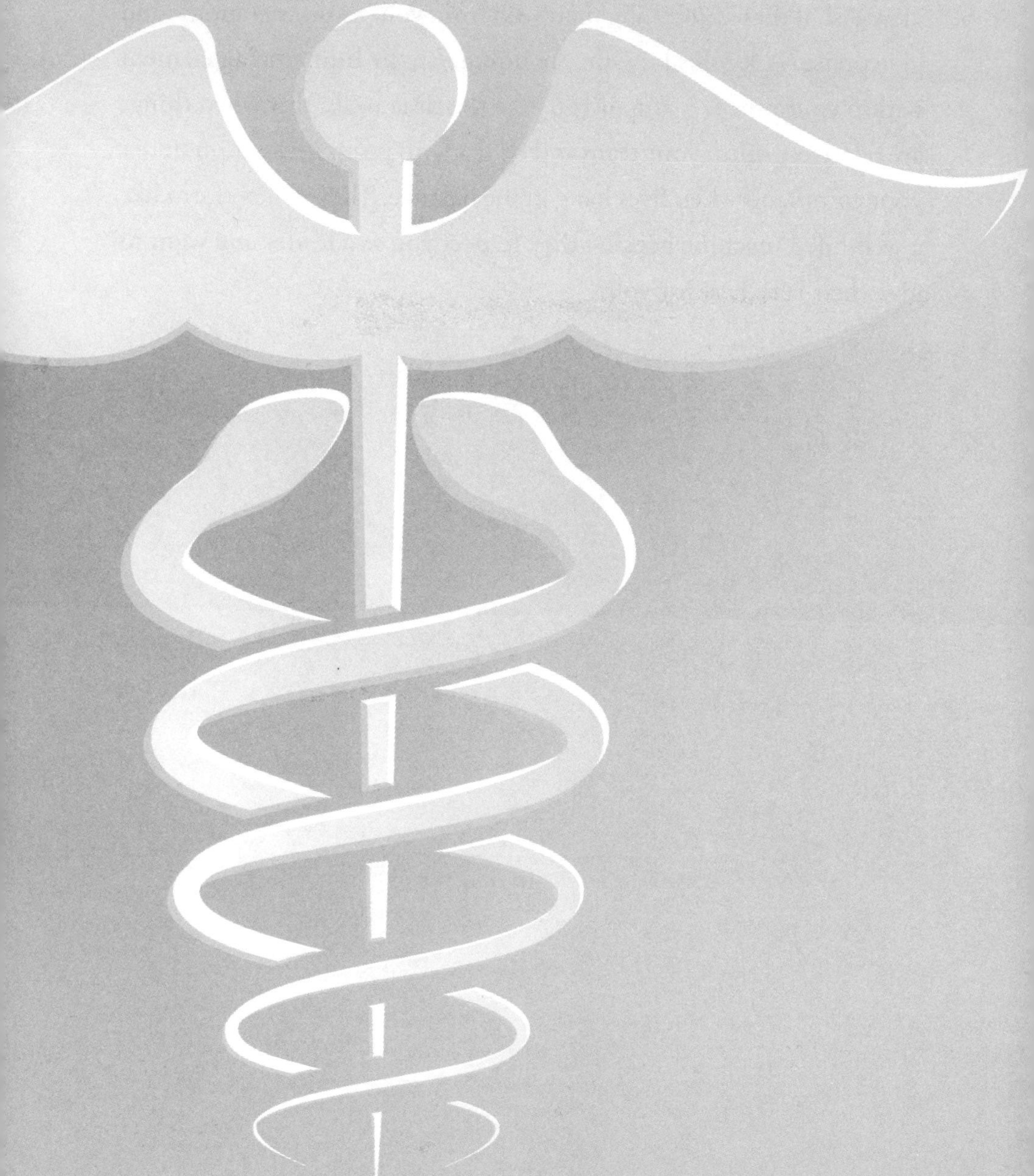

CHAPTER 3

Benefits of Better Leadership

True leadership lies in guiding others to success. In ensuring that everyone is performing at their best, doing the work they are pledged to do and doing it well.

- BILL OWEN

Leadership Scenario 1

While being glared at intensely by a PGY-2 (a physician two years after graduating from medical school), a nurse makes an error during an ICU procedure. The patient's survival is briefly jeopardized, but the team quickly gets the situation under control, and the procedure is a success. Afterward, the PGY-2 says, "If you ever try to kill my patient again, I will f***ing kill YOU." The PGY-2 storms off without another word to anyone.

Leadership Scenario 2

A PGY-2 on his first day of a one-year rotation on an inpatient ward gathers the treatment team together and says, "Thank you all for coming. I know there has been a history of tension between the nurses and doctors, and between the administrative staff and doctors, on this ward. I am here to tell you I will do everything I can to change that over the next year. We are a team. We have the same goals. You deserve respect, and you will get it from me and from my team."

Physicians, almost without exception, are busy people. And much of our busyness revolves around pursuits we believe will improve health outcomes for our patients. In this book, I'm asking you to put in some extracurricular effort to learn skills you may not have been taught in medical school or elsewhere. Why should you invest the time and effort when your plate is already full? Why should you tackle this "leadership stuff" when you could be using the time to read medical journals and polish your technical skills?

The simple answer: better health outcomes for patients. And not in some nebulous future. The moment your leadership skills improve in the clinic or the operating room, you begin improving your patients' healthcare experience and health outcomes right now. And the better you get at leadership, the more improved results you will continue to see over time. This isn't abstract at all.

The process works something like this:

1. The physician has a "moment of truth" and realizes, *I am a leader. Right now. Leadership is an integral part of my job.*

2. The physician begins consciously developing leadership as a core competency.

3. The performance of the physician's healthcare teams improves— both immediately and in a gradual, sustainable way.

4. Patients are more comfortable and confident in the recommendations of the doctor and the practice, and more likely to make changes in behaviors.

5. Improved health outcomes for patients are seen—in the short term and the long term.

That's why we're doing this. Remember that big blank sheet of butcher paper I hung on my door? Nothing matters more to me—or probably to you—unless the end result is better outcomes for our patients.

But as I hope to show in this chapter, the benefits of improved physician leadership go beyond patient care. They cross over into personal and professional relationships.

Benefits at Every Level of Healthcare

Each of us has worked for good leaders and for not-so-great leaders, as the pair of vignettes above highlights. When have you performed better? When have you been more motivated? When have you been a better teammate, a better practitioner, a better member/leader of your organization?

Likely, the answer to all of the above was when you were part of a team with superior leadership. Good leadership motivates everyone and brings out everyone's best. When you know your work is valued, you strive to bring your A-game every day. When you know you are heard and respected, you want to participate more in decision-making. You feel empowered to help steer the ship and, when necessary, to raise your hand and say, "Hey, that doesn't make sense, why don't we try it this way?"

When you feel cared for by leadership, you want to care for your teammates and your leader in return. You cherish the camaraderie and the sense of mission you share, and you are willing to "take a bullet" for your teammates. Almost literally. Many of us saw this, day in and day out, during the height of COVID. Our team members were coming to work every day in what was essentially a war zone, putting their own lives at risk for our patients and one another. Outside of combat I've seldom seen such unity and dedication.

We have all experienced good leadership resulting in better teamwork. We also have seen when teamwork leads to better patient care, improved patient experience, and better patient outcomes. As I've said before, it is difficult to cite statistics that *prove* a causal relationship between physician leadership and patient health. Leadership is a many-faceted quality. It is difficult to quantify in measurable terms. Definitions vary. Past efforts to study the issue have been clouded by the fact that "physician leadership" is usually viewed in terms of identified leadership positions. Overall empirical data show mixed results as it is difficult to show a statistically significant causal effect of leader traits on patient outcomes with so many control, moderating, and mediating variables in all healthcare settings. This is the point in the book where I am asking you to reflect on your own experiences with excellent leaders and connect the dots to better patient outcomes—reinforced by the specifics below.

Reduction in Disruptive Physician Behavior

Teaching physicians that they are leaders, from the start of medical school, will almost certainly result in a substantial decrease in disruptive physician behavior. Much of the current disruptive behavior stems, I believe, from an identity disconnect. Many physicians simply don't identify themselves as leaders but rather as members of the "frontline" treatment team (which they are, too, of course). When they behave disruptively, they are almost always doing so in passionate defense of their patients' health. The physician in Scenario 1 at the start of the chapter, for example, was no doubt reacting out of pure emotion after his patient's health was jeopardized. He was also attempting to *influence thought and behavior to achieve a desired result*—better performance from the nurse—but was not doing so in an effective, sustainable (or acceptable) way.

Had he internally *identified* himself as a leader, however, he would likely have kept his behavior better in check. He would have taken a step back and thought about a more effective way to influence his teammate. Part of his prior leadership training would have been scenario-based and tailored to situations like the one he experienced and his response in that training would have been part of the assessment of his suitability to graduate and become a doctor.

We all possess a natural ability to shift our behavior based on the role we are playing at any given moment. We act differently when we are teachers than when we are students, or when we are playing parent as opposed to son or daughter. We shift our behavior when we are sellers as opposed to buyers. We behave in accordance with the expectations of the role. When "leader" becomes engrained in the identity of physicians, doctors will adjust their behavior accordingly.

As all doctors come to see themselves as leaders, leadership skills will be infused into every level of medicine, as we see in the military. Part of the challenge in medicine right now is that when disruptive physician behavior occurs, the response is from peers and bosses who themselves may not have received much formal leadership training. And so, when a physician starts yelling, other physicians might yell back, which accomplishes little and can elevate the adrenaline level in the room. Or the boss may adopt a punitive stance and say, "Don't you ever act like that again on my unit! One more stunt like that and you are suspended."

Instead, let's envision a healthcare system where all physicians are trained in leadership skills. In most cases, these physician leaders will have the self-awareness not to lapse into emotional outbursts in the first place. In those instances where emotion still gets the better of them, their peers and leaders will handle them with greater wisdom. Being trained as leaders themselves, they may, instead of yelling back, take the disruptive physician aside and say, "What's going on, Ann? You're not yourself today. Let's sit down and chat for a few minutes." Or they may provide a bit of on-the-spot coaching.

Think about a baseball player swinging as hard as they can at every pitch and missing. Their goal is to score and help the team. They have energy, desire, and commitment. But their current actions are proving ineffectual. What they need is a coach to take them aside and tell them, "Instead of a full swing, try a three-quarter swing." They can then change their stance, and pretty soon they're belting doubles and triples. What disruptive physicians need is to be shown a more sustainable and effective way to get what they are looking for—a high-performing team and exceptional patient care.

Higher Performance in Teams

Good leadership translates to higher-performing teams, the gold standard we all strive for in healthcare.

I had the privilege, during the COVID-19 crisis, to see high performance in action. The situation we faced in hospitals every day was dire. We didn't know how lethal the virus was to us. We were watching patients get sick and die, and we didn't know the best protocols to use. None of this had ever been done before. Some interventions worked, some didn't. And the uncertainty was monumentally stressful. Were we doing the right things?

On top of that, there was no end in sight. We couldn't tell ourselves, "Just push yourself for two more weeks and it'll be over." We had no idea when, or even if, the pandemic would end. It reminded me of US Army Ranger training. One of the psychological games the Ranger Instructors would play was to load us up with 110 pounds of gear and take us on forced marches. We'd march down a road for five miles, then turn around and march back. And just as we were approaching camp, ready to offload our packs, they'd turn and march us down another road for three or four miles. Then we'd head back toward camp, and they'd do it to us again. Not knowing when the challenge is going to end is a tremendous mental stressor.

And yet, as tired and scared as team members were in our hospital, their performance on many measures ranked at the very top of the nation and the planet. I was reminded of situations like combat and the Apollo 13 mission. When you put a good team in a tremendously challenging and difficult environment, with good leadership at all levels of the organization, they can actually thrive and do some of the best work anyone has ever seen.

There were also teams that didn't perform well under COVID. According to a report by the National Library of Medicine (part of the National Institutes of Health):

> During the 2020 global pandemic crisis, some health care teams pulled together while others fell apart. The teams who pulled together put aside their differences and became stronger, putting their patients first and then each other. Those teams grew stronger, but some teams completely fell apart. They spent their days nitpicking, complaining, and arguing— making decisions based on what was best for themselves, not patients or their coworkers. The common denominator in determining how well teams performed was the leader. Employees looked to their leaders to successfully lead them through crisis, whether it was on a small or global scale.[5]

Does this quote not encapsulate everything this book is saying?

What do high-performing teams look like?

What are some qualities that characterize high-performing teams? First, there is a rhythm, a cadence to their work. A palpable sense of flow. Everyone is fully present to their tasks and working in sync with their teammates. As in a long-time marriage, teammates can finish each other's sentences or communicate changes in plans with a simple glance or nod of the head.

---

5   Renee Thompson and Mitchell Kusy, "Has the COVID Pandemic Strengthened or Weakened Health Care Teams? A Field Guide to healthy Workforce Best Practices," Nurs Adm Q, Apr-Jun 2021, doi: 10.1097/NAQ.0000000000000461. PMID: 33570881.

We see examples of this in sports—the blind, behind-the-back pass in basketball, the change of play at the line of scrimmage in football. Julian Edelman, when he was with the New England Patriots, often said that Tom Brady could just give him a look and he would change the route he was running. They were high performers, at the top of their game.

Another thing you notice about high-performing teams is that teammates take care of one another. They *want* to be together, doing the things they do well. Someone will say to a nurse after a long day in the ICU, "Hey, I'm here to relieve you," and the nurse will say, "No, I'll stay and finish this one up." People are engaged and motivated to see their work through to the end. They strive to go above and beyond. They come in early and stay late, because there's no place they'd rather be than with their teammates, saving lives. There's a feeling of excitement and privilege from being on the team. When new people sub in, they immediately catch the high-performance feeling too.

What do low-performing teams look like?

A low-performing team has an entirely different feel and rhythm.

In low-performing teams, there may be a lot of yelling, anger, and frustration. Tension hangs in the air, and people walk on eggshells, worried about "setting off" teammates or the leader. Actions become tentative and hesitant. Errors occur. Teammates overthink their actions. They lose confidence in their decision-making. They lose sight of any correlation between their actions and the outcomes they are experiencing. They ask a lot of questions too—which in itself is not a bad thing but can be an indicator that people are questioning their own expertise and judgment. When you see highly experienced healthcare professionals beginning to doubt themselves, it could be a sign that a team is in trouble.

Another hallmark of low-performing teams is apathy. *Quiet quitting* is a term that has crept into the current vernacular. It describes a situation wherein employees haven't physically left their jobs but have moved on internally. They're doing just enough not to get fired. Quiet quitting is contagious in the absence of good leadership. And when several people on your team start mailing it in, it stands to reason that the team's performance will suffer.

Leadership is the key differentiator

What is it, then, that separates low-performing teams from high-performing teams? We could probably name a dozen differentiators, but three come to my mind immediately: trust, caring, and longevity. And all three of these factors stem directly from strong leadership.

Trust

Stephen M. R. Covey's excellent book, *The Speed of Trust* (2006), points out how quickly and efficiently things can happen in an organization where trust exists. In one example, Warren Buffet signed off on a multibillion-dollar deal based on a two-hour meeting and a handshake because he knew and trusted the teams in the negotiation. By contrast, when trust doesn't exist, the two sides can take weeks or months to agree on a two hundred-page contract because teams are hyper-analyzing every clause. We have all experienced the speed of trust and the slowness of distrust. When we trust in ourselves, in our teammates, and in our leaders, decisions are made rapidly and executed with the fluidity of a finely tuned machine. Conversely, when trust is absent, we doubt ourselves and we need to double- and triple-check every element of every decision. This is enormously time-consuming and draining.

Caring

In high-performing healthcare teams, there is a palpable sense that people care *about* each other and *for* each other, in addition to caring for the patient. It is the sense of being cared for and caring for others that fuels teams through difficult periods and spurs them to want to excel.

Time spent together

High performance in teams is also a function of time spent together. That's just common sense. The longer a team works together, the better they get to know one another's habits, rhythms, responses, and thought patterns. Conversely, it's hard to develop high performance in a team when key members continually quit to seek greener pastures.

Good leadership is a key component in building trust and creating a sense of caring in a team. And when people experience these two elements, they are motivated to stick around long enough to develop the synchronization and muscle memory that marks high-performance teams.

High performance, in turn, creates high morale and satisfaction for the team, and this is the environment in which patients thrive.

Happier, More Well-Rounded Physicians

Most of us know physicians who are accomplished in their fields but whose home lives or interpersonal relationships are less than optimal. These people are often extremely intelligent, caring, and good-hearted, but they have simply not put enough focus on the "soft skills" of life: empathy, emotional intelligence, and relationship-building. Often "type A" personalities, they pushed themselves through college, medical school, and residencies with a single-minded, laser focus on becoming the best physician possible. Meanwhile, they had personality or character flaws that weren't being addressed. Eventually they find themselves failing in the realm of human relationships.

Leadership training doesn't let you get away with this. It begins with improving your self-awareness (as we'll see in the next chapter), and it proceeds to developing a set of people-skills that are just as transformative in nonwork relationships as they are in the office—listening, communicating, caring, conflict resolution, cultural competency.

Being a better leader is, in many ways, synonymous with being a better human being. As you practice the "soft skills" of leadership with your children, your spouse, your friends, and your neighbors, you improve all your nonwork relationships. The quality of your life becomes richer. You bring that happier, improved self back to the hospital or clinic—which further enhances your work relationships in a virtuous cycle that touches every aspect of your life and work.

Better business skills too

Leadership training can also involve developing skills and knowledge in some of the more administrative and business-oriented aspects of the job, such as human resource management, healthcare finance, or strategic thinking. A trained physician leader not only gains more competency in these areas but also learns how to better understand the team members who handle the nonclinical aspects of running a practice or a clinic.

Doctors today face increasing burdens in meeting insurance-related and regulatory requirements. The amount of paperwork has ballooned in recent years. This is not a minor issue, nor is it unrelated to physicians' happiness and mental health. A 2019 Medscape survey of 15,000 physicians found that 44 percent of doctors were experiencing burnout. When asked the reasons for this, "too many bureaucratic tasks" was far and away the number one response, followed, in order, by "spending too many hours at work," "increas[ed] computerization of practice (electronic medical/ healthcare records or EMRs/EHRs)," and "lack of respect from administrators/employees, colleagues or staff."[6]

Patient-related reasons barely cracked the top ten list.

It is not hard to see that doctors today feel overwhelmed—and *diminished*—by bureaucratic demands. Many feel their clinical judgment no longer counts as much as it once did. One solution many consider is to resign from medicine. A better solution, perhaps, is for physicians to gain more expertise and confidence in the administrative aspects of the job, so they feel more like empowered participants. A good program in physician leadership should give physicians the basic management tools they need to streamline the nonclinical aspects of the job, as well as the confidence to intelligently push back against non–value-added insurance and regulatory requirements that detract from patient care.

As physicians become more business-literate, we can expect to see less burnout, smoother operations for patients and staff, and less tension between physicians and the bureaucracies with which they are compelled to interact.

Organizational Benefits

Healthcare organizations are also prime beneficiaries of better physician leadership—not just as practiced by titled leaders but as practiced by all staff physicians.

---

6   Advisory Board, Physician Burnout in 2019, Uncharted, January 18, 2019, https:// www.advisory.com/daily-briefing/2019/01/18/burnout-report.

Improved patient satisfaction and financial results

As I will continue to emphasize throughout this book, better physician leadership leads to better patient outcomes. Closely tied to improved outcomes is improved patient *satisfaction*, as reflected in patient surveys and online reviews. This is good for hospitals' bottom lines. As a 2021 article in *Medical Economics* puts it:

> Studies... show a direct correlation between patient experience and profitability. ...[P]ositive patient experience is associated with increased profitability, and a negative patient experience is even more strongly associated with decreased profitability. Furthermore, patients' quality perceptions have accounted for a 17% to 27% variation in key financial metrics, and negative word of mouth about a hospital or health system could result in revenue losses up to $400,000 over one patient's lifetime.[7]

In short, patient satisfaction matters. Value-based reimbursement is becoming increasingly common in medicine, especially since the passage of the Affordable Care Act in 2010. Patient satisfaction is being routinely captured in surveys such as the HCAHPS (Hospital Consumer Assessment of Healthcare Providers and Systems). High scores in the HCAHPS are not only being used to competitively attract more patients to hospitals and other facilities; they are also being used to set reimbursement rates.

Hospitals now have a direct financial incentive to improve patients' experiences, and one of the best ways to do this is at the granular level: ensure that every physician in the organization is practicing excellent leadership skills with their colleagues, their teams, their patients, and their patients' families.

---

7   Michael Blackman, MD, "The Link between Financial Success and Patient Satisfaction, Medical Economics, July 3, 2021, https://www.medicaleconomics.com/view/the-link-between-financial-success-and-patient-satisfaction.

Better staff retention

As I mentioned earlier, "people join organizations, but they leave bosses." A main reason people quit their jobs is dissatisfaction with the leaders. Conversely, when bosses have well-honed leadership skills, people want to work for them and stick around.

Staff turnover has always presented a problem for organizations, but particularly so in this era of the Great Resignation. Attracting and retaining top staff is a concern for every healthcare organization, and turnover is a huge problem. First, there are the direct costs of recruiting and hiring new staff. Cost estimates for replacing midlevel healthcare employees range as high as 150 percent of annual salary.[8] According to *dailypay*, "The RN turnover rate in 2021 stood at 27.1%. The average cost of turnover for a bedside RN is more than $46,000, costing the average hospital between $5.2 million and $9 million per year."[9]

Then there are the indirect costs, such as decreased morale. One of the main reasons people feel connected to their jobs is the relationships they develop with coworkers whom they consider friends. As these coworkers quit and job relationships dwindle, so does workers' sense of connection to their jobs.[10] When there is heavy employee turnover, people become disengaged and are much more likely to quit, further exacerbating the problem.

We can also add the principle discussed above: developing high-performance teams requires time spent together. Excellence is attained when motivated, talented people work together for long periods and

---

8   DailyPay, "Understanding Employee Turnover in the Healthcare Industry," accessed September 10, 2023, https://www.dailypay.com/resource-center/ebooks/guide-to-employee-turnover-in-the-healthcare-industry/.

9   Ibid.

10   Kathy Gurchiek, "Survey: Workplace Friends Important Retention Factor," SHRM, December 2014, accessed July 25, 2023, https://www.shrm.org/resourcesandtools/hr-topics/employee-relations/pages/workplace-friendships.aspx.

develop caring relationships and complementary skills—along with that mysterious ability to communicate volumes with a word or a look in the eye.

Good leadership at every organizational level is the key to staff retention.

Better relationships between physicians and administrators

Historically, there has been some tension between physicians and hospital management, which has not served healthcare well. While there are notable exceptions, physicians typically have excellent clinical knowledge but, for the most part, little formal management training. The people who run most hospitals, on the other hand, typically have business or healthcare administration degrees and years of experience running hospitals but limited clinical expertise.

These gaps can become more apparent when physicians are placed in senior executive roles. The physician may feel like a fish out of water. Accustomed to making authoritative decisions and writing orders, the physician soon finds things don't work that way in organizational life. Listening, compromising, delegating, and influencing are vital skills. Lack of understanding of basic business, finance, and management principles becomes a handicap. Making structured, progressive leadership development an integral part of physicians' education can help to shrink this gap and give healthcare organizations the confidence to hire more physicians in senior executive roles.

Leadership developed for physicians should improve relations between physicians and hospital executives. If you've never acted as a leader or given much thought to how difficult leadership is, it's easy to throw stones at higher-ups and say, "*You need to do better.*"

But if you have worked in leadership yourself, you develop a greater level of empathy—even sympathy—for the leaders in your organization. Instead of reflexively talking badly about administrators, you recognize they are only human, and they have resource constraints, experience constraints, and expertise constraints. That gives you the *æquinimitas* to say, "Okay, the situation may not be ideal, but I'm going do everything I can to make it better from where I stand."

Better succession scenarios

Consistent leadership training for physicians will also result in a better succession pool for healthcare organizations. Hospitals will be able to choose from numerous qualified internal candidates who have ten, twelve, or fifteen years of leadership training and experience under their belts. The jump from doctor to executive will seem more natural. Healthcare organizations will be able to develop robust succession plans that take full advantage of their physicians' clinical expertise.

We've looked at why improved physician leadership will produce better outcomes across the healthcare landscape; now, let's look at how we can accomplish this.

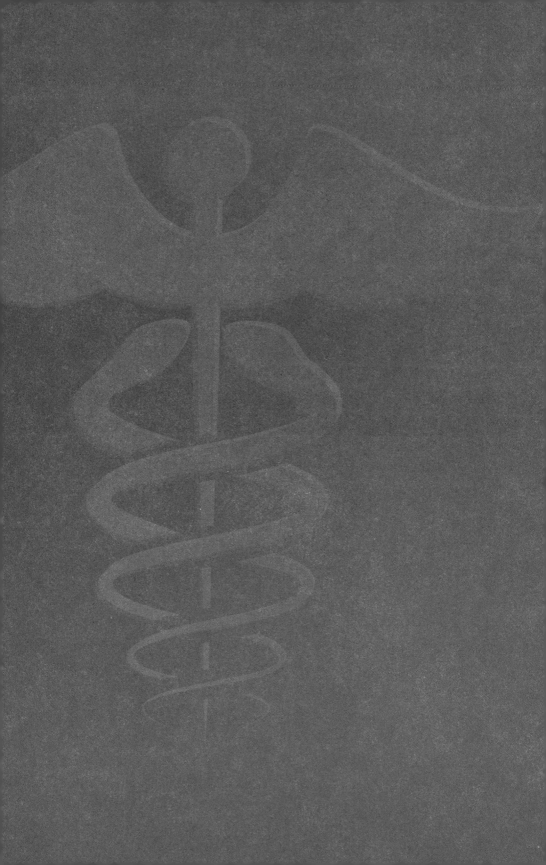

A Proposed Leadership Development Model:

The Concentric
Circles of Leadership

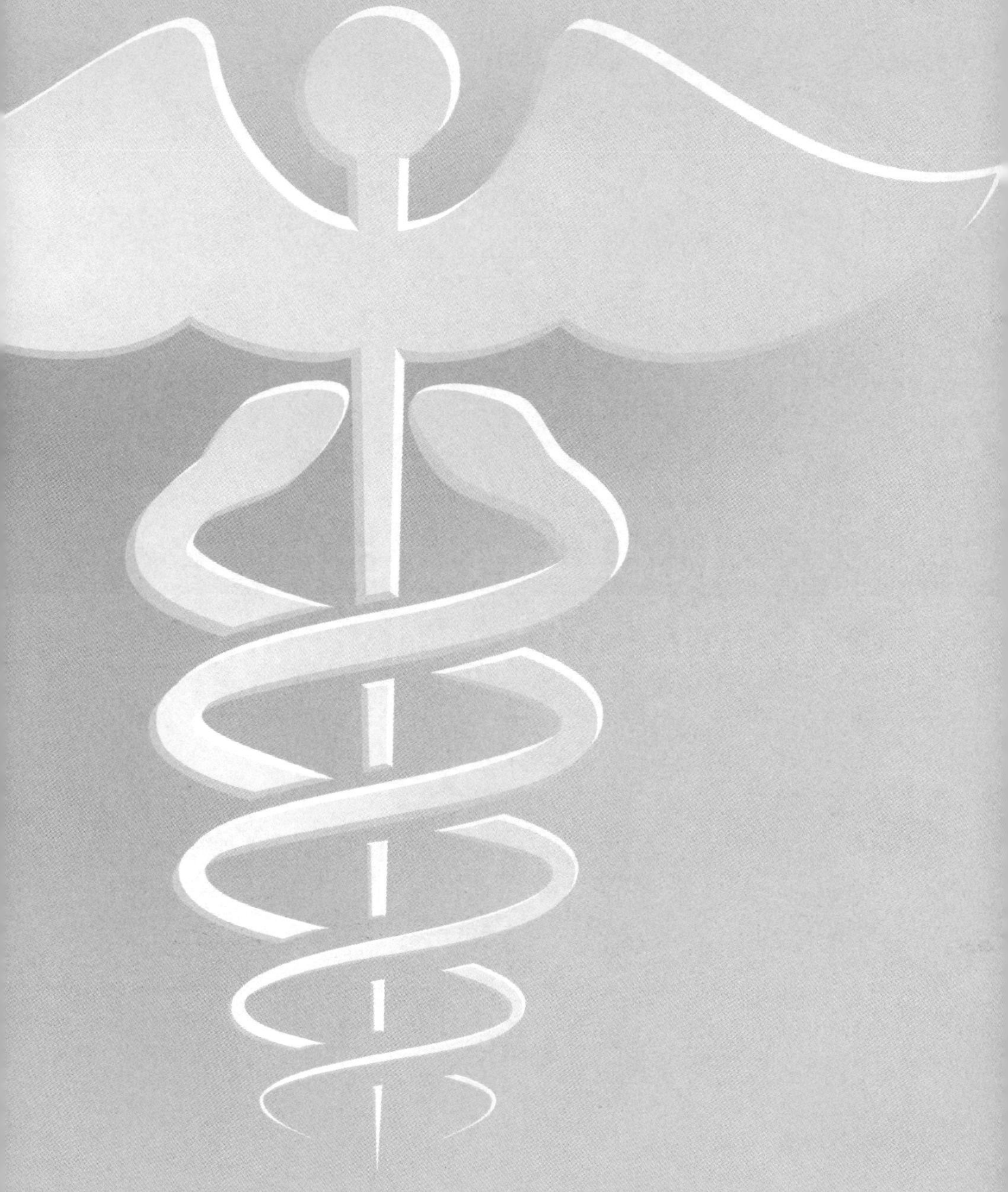

CHAPTER 4

Leadership Circle #1:

Leading Yourself

It is absurd that a man should rule others
who cannot rule himself.

- LATIN PROVERB

Leadership Scenario 1

A physician has had a very busy night, with little to no sleep. She is not feeling her best, to put it mildly, when she arrives in the clinic in the morning. The first patient's prep work is already running late—it's taking an extra fifteen minutes to get their vital signs and insurance paperwork done. The doctor realizes, we're running behind, right out of the starting gate. This day will not go well. She sees a nurse and a tech standing in the hallway, laughing, and says to them in a thickly sarcastic tone, "It's good to see some of us have extra time on our hands." She opens her office door and adds, "I'll just wait in here until you have the first patient ready." She enters the office and shuts the door loudly.

Leadership Scenario 2

The same situation. A physician has been up all night and enters her clinic in the morning not feeling her best. She sees her team members getting ready for the day—the front desk associate, a couple of medical assistants, a nurse. She announces, "Good morning. Can I talk to you all for a sec?" Everyone gathers outside her office, and she says, "Hey look, I was up all night. I'm tired, and I'm not at the top of my game. I'd appreciate all of you helping me out. If you see me doing something that doesn't seem right or if I act short with someone, please take me aside and point that out. Okay? Thanks so much. Now let's get these patients taken care of."

In the first section of this book, I argued that a new mindset is needed in medicine, one in which we view all physicians as the leaders they inherently are and begin training them in leadership as a core competency. But most importantly, *we need all physicians to view themselves as the leaders they inherently are.* I hope I've shown you some of the benefits we can expect to reap when doctors fully adopt their leadership role.

In this part of this book, we will get into the *how*. Through my years of observing and mentoring physician leaders in the armed forces, and later in civilian healthcare settings, I've found the model below a very useful framework for personal leadership development.

The Concentric Circles of Leadership

Leadership development can be viewed as a series of concentric circles that build upon one another and constantly reinforce one another, like the rings of a tree trunk.

The circles "grow" from the center outward. As with a tree trunk, the inner circle must be strong before you can start adding to it and before it can support growth. But as the outer circles develop, they, in turn, add strength back to the center.

Unlike with a tree, the center is never "done," and you don't need to "complete" one circle before moving to the next. All the circles inform one another, back and forth, in constant dynamic interaction. But conceptually, beginning at the all-important center is optimal.

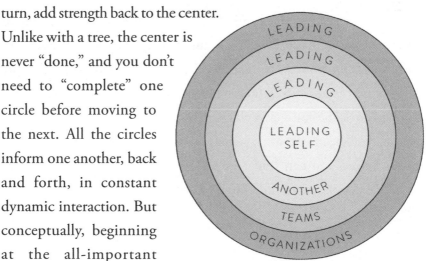

The Concentric Circles of Leadership.

Circle 1: Leading yourself

The core circle, the one upon which all the others build, is leading yourself. As the opening quote for this chapter suggests, it is impossible to lead others effectively if you cannot lead yourself. As a physician, you have already demonstrated that you have the focus and self-discipline to lead yourself through medical school and to develop the high-level skills required to be a practicing medical doctor. Can you now develop the personal competencies that would optimize your ability to lead your treatment team so your patients receive the best possible care? Can you learn through reflection what your leadership tendencies are and whether they are the most effective option in the varied environments of healthcare? It all starts with you. In so doing, you also become the model of leadership behavior others can emulate with success. It isn't fair to ask another person (Circle 2) to exhibit traits and skills you are not willing and able to develop in yourself.

Circle 2: Leading another

The next circle of leadership is the ability to influence individuals on a one-to-one basis. Circle 2 leans heavily on Circle 1 and progresses directly from it. It includes many of the "soft skills" that are often taught in medical school—although usually without sufficient emphasis or cohesion—as well as many that are not. To lead another person, you need empathy, listening skills, presentation skills, and more. Before you can lead teams (Circle 3), you must be able to influence people on an individual basis.

Circle 3: Leading teams

Circle 3 flows from Circle 2. Leading a team of twelve is really leading twelve individuals. A group leadership event is just a collection of one-on-one leadership events bundled together. Each member of the group is listening and processing your leadership efforts through the lens of her/his experiences, level of interest, and degree of trust. If you have trouble leading one individual, it will be difficult to lead a team or a group. But leading groups also requires an added level of competence in areas such as team building and group dynamics. Knowing how to lead teams helps prepare you for Circle 4, Leading Organizations.

Circle 4: Leading organizations

Finally, to lead an organization means to lead a collection of teams, and teams consist of individuals. Everything you know about leading yourself, leading other individuals, and leading teams will be called into play when you lead on the large scale. If you can't shepherd your own thoughts and behaviors, you won't be able to influence another person's, and you certainly won't be able to successfully and consistently influence those of ten thousand individuals. Circle 4 success is supported by study and effort at Circles 1, 2, and 3.

But again, although the circles build one upon the other, this isn't a strictly linear process. In real life, things are messier and more dynamic. You will often be called upon to lead teams while you're still working on leading yourself and leading another. You'll probably still be learning how to lead teams when organizational leadership is thrust upon you. The outer circles inform the inner ones as well. So, it's not as if you need to master each circle before you can tackle the next one. The idea is that the circles support each other from inside out. And the more skill you develop in each circle, the better you will perform in the others, in a continuous back-and-forth process.

The concentric circles model can help you sort out leadership breakdowns at any stage. Let's say, for instance, you're an organizational leader and you've just given a talk to five hundred employees. Something about it didn't land right. Audience members were looking at their phones and squirming in their seats. Using the circles framework, you might ask yourself, *Was there a particular group I offended or excluded with my remarks (Circle 3)? Was there an individual I didn't respond to well when they asked a question (Circle 2)? Or was it just me having an off day (Circle 1)?* And then you can go and collect feedback from that team or that individual and try to correct whatever communication went awry. Or you can examine your own state of mind. What was affecting your performance? Can you learn to manage your emotions better next time?

Alternatively, you could take the attitude, *The audience was just a bunch of jerks. They should have been listening to me, but they weren't.* That's the easy—and thoroughly ineffectual—option. Taking full responsibility for outcomes is always the preferable response. And the concentric circles model gives you a tool for doing that.

In the four chapters of Section II, we'll look at each of the four circles. Naturally, Circle 1 comes first.

Circle 1: Leading Yourself

Every leadership event, every step in your growth as a leader, begins with you. Harkening back once again to our definition of leadership, you must be able to *influence your own thought and behavior toward desired results* if you wish to influence others. The very effort you are making right now to improve your leadership skills is a manifestation of this. You are striving to influence your own behavior to achieve a desired result—which is to be a better leader.

Self-leadership means you are able to assess your own strengths and weaknesses and to frequently reflect on your leadership performance. You are able to set goals, make sound decisions, and follow through on them, taking full ownership of your behavior each step of the way. It is a base requirement for those who would lead others. Ineffective leadership is usually traceable to problems in Circle 1. Why is it we often see people in leadership roles who struggle to lead themselves? One simple answer is that, on an organizational level, people typically get promoted to leadership positions as a reward. In medicine, for example, people may get promoted because of their research and grant portfolio, clinical expertise, revenue generation, or otherwise add value to the organization. But these people haven't necessarily *aspired* to be leaders, and so they often haven't done the inner work to develop themselves on that axis. Leadership is a distinct skillset, and again, it begins with the ability to lead yourself.

Self-leadership has several key components.

Self-awareness

The most fundamental aspect of self-leadership is self-awareness. You must have some knowledge of who you are before you can lead yourself—and then others. Many definitions of self-awareness exist, but most of them have two main components. Self-awareness involves (1) an ability to observe and understand your own thoughts, emotions, and behaviors, and (2) an ability to see yourself as others see you. And so, we might say that there are two aspects to self-awareness, internal and external.

Internal self-awareness

Many people go through life acting on their thoughts and emotions in a more-or-less automatic way. It doesn't occur to them that they have full authorship of their behavior. Habitually, they have a thought, which leads to an emotion, which leads to a behavior. An example might be a man who sees another man's name on his wife's cellphone. He becomes jealous. His jealousy quickly turns to rage. He storms into the other room and screams at his wife. He is following his impulses without stepping back and considering what kind of communication might help clarify misunderstandings. Disruptive physician behavior often occurs in a similar way.

Self-awareness, therefore, begins with a recognition that "I am not just my thoughts and behaviors." When you realize there is an aspect of yourself that is more fundamental than your mental and emotional activity, you begin to gain the ability to look at your thoughts and feelings more objectively and exercise more control over them. Internal self-awareness is a lifelong process that leads to an ever-deepening understanding of your own emotions and how to manage them. Over time, you begin to recognize your emotional triggers—the things that "set you off" in one way or another—and to learn about those areas of yourself that require more insight and growth. You gain the ability to evaluate yourself and make changes.

Self-awareness also involves consciously understanding what "makes you tick" as a person—your values, your passions, your preferences, your motivating and demotivating factors.

External self-awareness

External self-awareness is the ability to look at your behavior with a measure of objectivity and imagine the effect it is having on others. As you practice external self-awareness, you begin to ask questions such as *What message is my tone of voice and my body language conveying? Is my behavior aligned with my values? Is my behavior consistent with what I am trying to teach others? What effect will my mood likely have on the group?*

The more awareness you develop about your effect on others, the more you begin to exercise control over your behavior and learn new ways of behaving that are more consistent with the way you intend to influence others.

Self-awareness leads to...

The more self-awareness you gain, the more willing you are to accept responsibility for problematic situations that occur in your work and home life. Instead of automatically blaming others, you strive to understand the role you played. I once saw a t-shirt that read, "Has it ever occurred to you that the only thing all your dysfunctional relationships have in common is you?"

If you are a highly self-aware person, you accept responsibility for every event and circumstance in your life. That doesn't mean you hold others faultless, but it does mean you take full responsibility for the part you undoubtedly played in the situation, either by your current actions, your past actions, or your lack of action.

Self-awareness gives you a road map of the inner terrain you need to work on to become a better leader and a better person. Without self-awareness, you simply don't embark on that challenging journey.

As you gain self-awareness, you also gain greater awareness of other people. You understand *their* behavior better, and you gain more compassion for them. This is an essential aspect of becoming a leader.

Developing self-awareness

Self-awareness is a trait we value highly in leaders, friends, and peers. We are drawn to self-aware people because they tend not to be an [insert seven-letter word starting with "a"]. We want to follow self-aware people. We want them on our teams.

And yet our current healthcare culture, oddly enough, doesn't teach self-awareness. We *hope* people will develop it on their own, but we don't require it or provide a road map. Thus, it is not uncommon for highly intelligent people to live well into adulthood—or to live their entire lives—without developing much self-awareness. This can be especially true for people who have an intense and busy external focus, such as doctors-in-training (who later become doctors-in-practice). We have all known, and worked for, physicians who, despite decades of career success, appear to have spent little time developing awareness of their leadership style or its impact on others.

The first step, then, to developing self-awareness is simply to realize what it is and to recognize its importance as a goal and begin working toward it. That step alone—the desire to develop self-awareness and writing it down as a personal goal—is 60 percent of the battle, and it's a step many people never take.

The next step is to do the actual work.

Do a self-inventory/self-assessment

In twelve-step programs, step number four is to make "a searching and fearless moral inventory of ourselves." Doing an internal inventory of some kind is a wise endeavor for every adult, not just recovering addicts. At some point in life, especially if you intend to be a leader, you need to take stock of who you are, what matters to you, what your strengths and weaknesses are, and the legacy you intend to create through your presence on planet Earth.

Evaluating yourself isn't a discrete, one-time event—it can and should be spread out over a lifetime—but formalizing the work, in a way that feels right for you, can be powerful. For example, you might spend a few days alone in a cabin, in quiet contemplation, without books, electronics, or other distractions. You might work with a coach or sign up for an intensive workshop. Or you might take a written self-assessment. Whatever method you use, your self-inventory should include probing questions such as:

- What are my core values? What do I care about more than anything?

- What are my moral principles? Do I live by them?

- What are my greatest character strengths and weaknesses?

- What do I view as my purpose in life?

- How would I rate my own leadership qualities and abilities?

- What is my effect on others? What traits do I model by my behavior?

- Would I want to work for myself as a boss? Why or why not?

- What are my greatest personality challenges?

- What are my self-imposed limits? Where am I holding myself back from growth?

Seek feedback from others

The next part of gaining self-awareness is to seek feedback from the people who know you and work with you. Try to have methods in place for regularly collecting feedback on your skills and performance from peers, subordinates, mentors, patients, patients' families, and bosses. But also, and perhaps more importantly, continually seek it in an informal way.

Feedback from the people you lead is the most important. It's vital that you find a way to create psychological safety so that team members can give you feedback fearlessly and honestly. Here again, the idea of psychological size comes into play. Physicians have a certain stature that tends to create a "sphere of diffidence" around them. And when they have supervisory status over others this effect is magnified. When someone depends on you for their salary and livelihood, it is very difficult for them to give you honest feedback.

I remember back when I was privileged to be given command of a rifle platoon in the 82nd Airborne Division, one of America's premier military units. I was a brand-new second lieutenant infantry officer, and part of my new job was to do evaluations of my senior noncommissioned officers. These included a platoon sergeant and four squad leaders who, among the four of them, had over forty years of infantry experience, and I had barely over forty days! Their collective knowledge dwarfed mine.

You can learn more about leadership from the people you lead than from your boss.

I recognized this as a great learning opportunity for me, as I've always believed you can learn more about leadership from the people you lead than from your boss. After field training exercises I would gather the five of them in a room, and I'd ask them, "How did I do? How was my leadership? What can I do better?" But of course, as their officer, I had a lot of authority over these men, as well as the power to impact their careers through my written evaluations.

And so, the first couple of times I asked, they gave me answers like, "Oh, you were great, sir. That was awesome. Nothing to improve on." Sure.

My attitude was, "This was my first exercise. There must be things I can do better." I really wanted their honest feedback, but it took three or four iterations of this process before one of them finally ventured to say, "Well, sir, you kind of stepped on it with Corporal Otis. That wasn't great, the way you handled that. Correcting him for doing that is really his team leader's job, and you should let the chain of command do its job."

My response? An enthusiastic, "Thank you, Staff Sergeant. This is exactly what I need to hear." And this was a crucial reaction. If I had become defensive or given him any reason whatsoever to regret his candor, I would have set the process back another three months.

The people on your team possess valuable information about your leadership. You must demonstrate not only a *willingness* to accept feedback, but almost an *eagerness*. Your response to feedback should be something like, "Thank you. That's a great point. And I'm going to work on that. I'm glad you spoke up." You must accept feedback in a way that encourages more feedback.

And remember, you're simultaneously teaching leadership to others. You're *influencing their thought and behavior* so that they, too, will want to ask others for feedback.

When it comes to soliciting feedback from patients and/or families, you can ask for it in written form or you can have a staff person say to your patients, "Dr. S. is always trying to improve her skills with patients, so she wants to know, was there anything she could have done better? Anything you tell us will be completely anonymous."

As you gather feedback from others, ask yourself how well it correlates with your self-assessment. Does it reinforce what you already know about yourself? Does it diverge from your self-image?

It is also important to identify stimuli that affect you. Whenever you walk away from an encounter feeling uncomfortable, recognize this as a particularly important opportunity for reflection. *Why do I feel uncomfortable? When during the encounter did I begin to feel this? What were the words, body language, environmental cues that affected me? Do these same cues routinely "activate" me? What is my responsibility here? Should I reach out to others who may have been made uncomfortable? When? How?*

Develop a practice

Finally, it's important to have a *practice* for continuing to develop your self-awareness. Self-awareness is like physical fitness. There are countless ways to develop it, depending on your personal beliefs and inclinations. For example:

- Daily meditation/contemplation
- Counseling—both formal and informal
- Supervision or mentorship
- Reading self-development books, taking courses, etc.
- Guided retreats

Some prefer a self-guided method; others do better when an external structure or discipline is provided. The method is up to you, but it's important that you work on your self-awareness regularly, so that it becomes a habit. If you don't take the work seriously, it won't *influence your thought and behavior to achieve desired results.* Developing self-awareness is uncomfortable by its very nature, and everyone struggles with this. But, like regular exercise, it gets easier the longer you do it. As you begin to see the benefits, such as improved relationships, your efforts are rewarded and your defenses go down.

A growth mindset

As an adjunct to self-awareness, leaders can benefit from developing, or nurturing, what author and researcher Carol Dweck calls a "growth mindset," as opposed to a "fixed mindset."[11]

People with a fixed mindset tend to believe we human beings "are what we are." Our traits and capabilities are largely innate. The amount of talent, intelligence, and capacity we are born with is essentially our allotment for life, and all we can do is make the best of it. People with a fixed mindset say things like, "I'm good at organization, I'm bad with people." A fixed mindset is like having a cap on your capabilities. It discourages you from developing new skills and talents and tends to make you defensive, even arrogant, about the skills you already possess.

A growth mindset, on the other hand, is the belief that human beings can continue to develop new skills and capabilities throughout life. Growth-minded people believe there are no built-in limits to what they can learn and how they can change. They see themselves as perennial "works-in-progress" and know they will never be "finished." They are always trying to improve themselves. They love feedback. They believe every failure contains a lesson for growth. They embody Nelson Mandela's famous quote, "I never lose. I either win or learn."

> *I never lose.*
> *I win or I learn.*
> – NELSON MANDELA

Growth-minded leaders do not try to prove to others what great leaders they are. Rather, they are humble and sponge-like, continually absorbing new information with the intention of becoming better leaders tomorrow than they are today. They know leaders are not born; they are made.

---

11   Carol S. Dweck, *Mindset: The New Psychology of Success* (New York: Random-house, 2007).

Confidence and humility

Leading yourself, particularly as a physician leader, calls for a blend of confidence and humility that might seem contradictory at first, but really isn't.

I remember an army billboard from years ago. It showed a soldier guarding the Tomb of the Unknown Soldier. He was standing at attention, perfectly still, to the point that snow had piled up on his hat and shoulders. Under the picture was the text (to the best of my memory):

| *Pride /prīd/ noun: justifiable self-delight in one's accomplishments* |

Pride, interestingly, can signify a failing or a virtue. In fact, one dictionary definition of pride is "unjustified delight in one's achievements." But the army, in its ad, was clearly trying to stress the importance of pride in oneself as a virtue.

We can extract a couple of valuable things from this definition. First of all, the word *justifiable*. You need to have confidence that you are 100 percent capable of doing the job that you do. And you must be able to back up that confidence. For example, I cut people open for a living, an act that under different circumstances might land me in prison. I need to be able to walk into an operating room, place an eleven-day-old child on the table, open their skull, and remove a brain tumor, if necessary. It takes a certain level of confidence to be able to do that, and to reassure the parents that their baby is going to be okay. On the morning of surgery, significant self-doubt could be paralyzing. The child and her parents can't afford for me to lack sufficient confidence to do my job.

The second part of the definition is self-delight. You can and should take pride in your achievements. In short, it's *good* to feel *good* about the *good* things you've accomplished. But the delight you feel, notably, should be *self*-delight. You shouldn't need to hear it from others. You shouldn't need to brag about what you've done, how good you are, or where you earned your degree. Genuine, sustainable confidence flows from within, not without. In fact, if you find yourself seeking praise and validation from others—or worse, putting others down to make yourself feel better—that is a sure sign you don't have real confidence.

People often get this concept wrong. A doctor will march into a room and start shouting orders, making demands, treating people in a demeaning manner, and then storm out. And someone will say, "Wow he has such a big ego." Exactly the opposite is true, in my opinion. That kind of behavior is indicative of a very small "ego." Bullies and intimidators are people who feel insecure in themselves, and so they feel a constant need to bring other people down.

There are certainly insecure people in medicine (and in all fields). They're smart, they work hard, they get good grades, they get into a good medical school, and they become a surgeon (for instance), thinking all these things will make them feel good about themselves. But it turns out that feeling good about oneself doesn't derive from external things. It's all internal. And so, their insecurity continues unabated and often manifests as disruptive or arrogant behavior.

To lead most effectively you must go back to that center circle, reflect on it deeply, and optimize it. That doesn't happen by exhibiting dominance behaviors; it happens by developing quiet confidence and living within that confidence.

Confidence and humility are not opposites; they are joined at the hip. When you are confident in yourself, you don't need others to shore you up. Nor do you feel threatened by criticism. Your core is intact. So, when people give you "negative" feedback, you don't take it as a personal attack. Your growth mindset allows you to take it as helpful information that can improve your life and your leadership. That is the essence of humility.

Heeding a moral compass

An essential aspect of self-leadership—and, by extension, leading others—is to have a clear moral compass. That is, you know right from wrong, and you reliably do the right thing.

Note that the heading above reads, "*heeding* a moral compass," as opposed to *developing* a moral compass. I believe most of us—except, perhaps, sociopaths—already possess a solid moral compass by the time we reach adulthood. If we have two options in front of us, and one is right and the other wrong, we usually know which one is right. Our conscience tells us. We don't have to think about it for long. In fact, thinking about it for a long time is often a sign that we're trying to rationalize why doing the wrong thing might be okay. Selecting the right option is not complicated. *Doing* it may be difficult, but choosing it isn't often complicated.

> *When you reliably do the right thing, people begin to look to you for leadership, regardless of whether you are the CEO or a brand-new physician on the wards.*

Doing the right thing can be as small a matter as picking up a piece of trash in a hospital corridor (instead of rationalizing why we don't have time) or as consequential a matter as confronting a surgical peer whose drinking has begun to affect their work. When you're a leader—whether you're leading one person or fifty thousand—people look to you to make good moral and ethical choices. This stems from your ability to morally lead yourself.

Heeding a moral compass isn't only about choosing right over wrong, it's also about treating others with humanity. Just as we have a "voice" inside that knows right from wrong, we also have an impulse toward compassion, which we can choose to obey or disregard. Throughout the course of every day, we are presented with opportunities to offer help, speak a kind word, or give someone a bit of encouragement. When we follow the kind impulse—for example, stopping to give directions to a lost-looking hospital visitor—we inevitably feel better and make someone else feel better. We also model what a compassionate culture looks like.

When you reliably do the right thing, people begin to look to you for leadership, regardless of whether you are the CEO or a brand-new physician on the wards.

A sense of purpose

The ability to lead yourself is aided by having a sense of purpose. Just as companies have corporate mission statements to help guide their behavior, it is wise to have a personal mission statement, a clear sense of your "why." *Why do I do the work I do? What is it that gets me out of bed every morning and makes me eager to start my day?* Without a sense of a larger purpose to our daily actions, many of us burn out at some point. Human beings crave meaning; we want to be serving a purpose larger than ourselves.

In medicine, as I noted earlier, we are fortunate in that our mission couldn't be more honorable. We take care of people, often in times of great need, and we try to make their lives better and longer. We comfort families, we improve the health of our communities, and we improve the health of the world. Most people agree our mission is noble and straightforward. We improve health and save lives.

It's important to have a personally meaningful way that you frame your mission as a doctor and that you infuse yourself with that sense of mission daily. Don't allow yourself to become numbed by routine.

Know your mission and come to the clinic every day brimming with passion to fulfill it. A steadfast sense of purpose is what will carry you, and your team, through many a trying day.

Purpose is the spark that inspires others to follow you and to perform at a high level. Don't fail to remind yourself and your team of the mission on a regular basis. I try to do this often with my teams. I might just say to them, at the end of a day, "Think about what you did today. You made a difference in people's lives. Even if you were just handling paperwork or answering emails on the EMR system, you were easing patients' minds and making a difference in their lives. Don't ever lose sight of that."

By exuding purpose, you inspire team members to treat their daily work with the reverence and importance it merits. You are *influencing thought and behavior to achieve desired results*. And the results you are achieving are better patient outcomes through improved team member performance.

Practicing good self-care

Finally, a vital aspect of self-leadership is self-*care*. You can't care for others on a daily basis if you don't care for yourself. It is an overused metaphor, but one that applies nonetheless: on airline flights, we are reminded to put on our own oxygen mask before helping others with theirs. We are of no use to anyone else if we're passed out on the floor.

Being a physician is a demanding and stressful job. You must support your ability to perform it by taking care of yourself in the four domains of human life: physical, mental, emotional, and spiritual.

Physical fitness is essential, though easy to overlook when doing a job that seems primarily mental. Of course, as anyone who studies the brain knows, mental work consumes a great deal of physical energy.

That is why many top competitive chess players include physical workouts as part of their training. Stamina is also critical for long days on your feet. Personally, I try to work out regularly and participate in some form of athletics. I wouldn't be able to function well as a surgeon otherwise.

I recommend reading an article in the *Harvard Business Review*, written over twenty years ago, called "The Making of a Corporate Athlete," by Jim Loehr and Tony Schwartz. Loehr has spent a career studying performance and how it is optimized, among both elite athletes and corporate leaders, and has written several excellent books on the topic.

When training athletes for optimal performance, the authors notably "never focused on their primary skills—how to hit a serve, swing a golf club, or shoot a basketball. Likewise, in business we don't address primary competencies such as public speaking, negotiating, or analyzing a balance sheet. Our efforts aim instead to help executives build their capacity for what might be called supportive or secondary competencies, among them endurance, strength, flexibility, self-control, and focus. Increasing capacity at all levels allows athletes and executives alike to bring their talents and skills to full ignition and to sustain high performance over time—a condition we call the *Ideal Performance State* (IPS)."[12]

It is vital, as a leader in any field but particularly in medicine, to support your ability to be in IPS. And learning how to balance rest and recovery is an essential aspect of this. No Super Bowl-winning quarterback, no World Series-level pitcher is out there every day throwing balls, late into the night, then getting up early and doing it again. Top athletes understand the need to rest and get proper sleep

---

12 Jim Loehr and Tony Schwartz, "The Making of a Corporate Athlete," Harvard Business Review, January 2001, accessed September 15, 2023, https://hbr.org/2001/01/the-making-of-a-corporate-athlete.

and nutrition to optimize their performance. It's the variation, the oscillation, in their schedule that holds the key to excellence.

As physicians, our work culture is one of nonstop training and education for a decade or more, and then continued dawn-to-dusk work for decades thereafter. But as the article's authors point out, it is this very type of unrelenting push—this failure to oscillate—that creates suboptimal performance in the long run. Great athletes bring variety to their training and to their games. They have highly ritualized rest routines that are as vital to them as their periods of swinging a bat or a tennis racket. It is during these rest periods that they heal, gain strength, gather focus, and shake off negative thoughts. "Corporate athletes" who embrace periods of rest and variety have also been found to greatly increase their performance, as shown by external measures such as earning more income with less time in the office.

Taking care of yourself in the three nonphysical domains—mental, emotional, and spiritual—is equally important. When great athletes, and other successful professionals, describe their emotions during peak performance, they use words such as "calm," "optimistic," "focused," and "engaged."[13] These emotions feed us energy. Conversely, emotions such as "frustration, impatience, anger, fear, resentment, and sadness"[14] drain energy and hamper performance. So, it is important, during the course of each day, to find ways to recharge emotionally—for example, with music, laughter, taking deep breaths, going for walks, etc.—but also to work on having an emotionally healthy and rewarding home life.

Taking care of your mental and spiritual health is just as critical. Don't fall into the trap of saying, "I don't have time to [meditate, exercise, read a novel, take a long bath, walk in the woods...]." You

---

13   Ibid.

14   Ibid.

don't have time *not* to. These self-care activities, far from being distractions from your more important work, are the support system that allows you to do your highest-level work throughout a demanding twelve-hour (or longer!) day.

And now let's look at the next circle of leadership, Leading Another.

CHAPTER 5

Leadership Circle #2:

Leading Another

Become the kind of leader people would follow
voluntarily, even if you had no title or position.

- BRIAN TRACY

Leadership Scenario 1

A clinical team is preparing for a procedure—for example, a lumbar epidural steroid injection. The procedure room has been cleaned and prepped. The patient has been sedated and is on the table. A new technician stands by the instrument tray, ready to assist. Physician A, scrubbed and ready, walks in, looks at the instruments, and says, "Where's the 20-gauge Tuohy needle?"

The tech looks down at the tray, embarrassed, and says, "We don't have that in the clinic, Doctor."

The physician's jaw tenses. Red rises in his cheeks. "We've got a patient here, consented and sedated," he says, "and you're telling me we don't have the tools to do the job. Do you know what this means? Now we have to wake the patient, apologize, send her home, and hope she doesn't file a complaint. Why? Because you didn't do your job!"

Leadership Scenario 2

The same situation. Physician B asks for the instrument, and the new technician tells him they don't have it. The physician takes a deep breath and assesses the situation. He says to the technician, "I know you feel bad. This is your first month here. You haven't done one of these procedures before. But this isn't all on you. Clinic leadership and I should have checked this before the patient came in and was sedated. Yes, it would have been good if you had known I needed the Tuohy, but others should have known as well. Consider it a learning experience, for all of us. Next time, we'll do better as a team. Chin up."

The tech in Scenario 1 probably went outside and sat in her car for ten minutes, feeling terrible about herself and questioning her career choices. She will walk on eggshells around Physician A for the foreseeable future. The tech in Scenario 2, on the other hand, will probably be loyal to Physician B for life.

> *Leadership is about relationships with individual people, not cheering crowds.*

Leadership is composed of a long string of moments like the above. It is all about relationships with individual people, not cheering crowds. As you go through each day, the one-on-one moments and relationships add up to define who you are as a leader.

Leading Another Is Fundamental

Leading individual human beings is the fundamental unit of leadership. Although learning to lead yourself is essential, your ability to influence individuals, one at a time, determines your success as a leader. Anytime you're leading teams, departments, or entire organizations, you're actually leading individuals. For example, when I was standing in front of the forty infantrymen in my rifle platoon in the 82nd Airborne Division, everything I said was interpreted and processed by forty separate individuals. Each soldier was paired with me, the leader, in that dyadic, 1:1 interaction.

Your ability to form a positive relationship with another human being, even if you spend only five minutes with them, helps create a basis of caring and trust that allows you to *influence thought and behaviors to achieve a desired result*. On the other hand, every negative 1:1 interaction erodes your ability to lead.

Imagine walking into a procedure room and three of your five team members have had negative, anxiety-inducing experiences with you in the past. What do you suppose those three people will have said about you before you even entered the room? How do you think this will affect the other two teammates? The work atmosphere? The flow of the procedure? The confidence level of the team? How do you suppose it might affect *the patient's care*?

Now imagine the opposite. Three of the five people in the room have had positive experiences with you in which you supported and encouraged them. They like and respect you. They know you respect *them* and their abilities, too, and so they are primed to perform at the top of their game, rather than feeling nervous about making mistakes. They have likely communicated their positive opinion of you to the other two teammates. How do you think this team might perform during the procedure? How will this affect patient care?

Either version, repeated several thousand times, can be your career.

Leading individuals has an additive effect. Each person with whom you exert positive influence becomes an ally in your mission to provide exemplary healthcare to patients. These numbers add up steadily, especially when you consider that people are less likely to leave their jobs when they are happy with the leadership they experience.

Leadership of individuals also has a *multiplicative* effect. Your leadership, good or bad, influences the decision-making and behavior of each person you lead. This, in turn, informs their own leadership. Their leadership has a ripple effect, outward, on everyone with whom they come into contact. And so on, *ad infinitum*.

In addition, people talk. They talk about you when you're not in the room. Stories and opinions about physicians, both positive and negative, circulate throughout the workforce. And those opinions serve as the starting point of team members' attitudes toward you before they even meet you.

Staff talk to patients as well. When you walk into a patient room and the first thing the patient or their family member says is, "Oh, Doctor X, we've heard so many good things about you from the staff," you know your leadership is creating a positive multiplier effect. Nurses and technicians aren't paid to give spontaneous endorsements. They give them only when they feel personally motivated to do so.

Patients talk to one another, and to prospective patients, as well. Word of mouth spreads among the patient community, especially on social media. One motivated individual with a good or bad experience can capture the ear of thousands of would-be patients of yours. I've been fortunate, as have many of my colleagues, to receive the unsolicited endorsement of a number of online parent communities in our region (my practice is almost exclusively pediatric). Their heartfelt recommendations of me have been humbling and have undoubtedly brought many new patients through my doors.

As anyone in the advertising industry can tell you, this is the type of publicity "money can't buy." Word-of-mouth recommendations, given freely and spontaneously by users of your services, are far more powerful than any type of paid advertising—because they are shared without personal benefit to the sharer. And the sharer puts their credibility on the line.

I don't mean to reduce this to a commercial consideration. Think about how such word of mouth can affect your ability to lead patients. You are, after all, trying to *influence their thought and behavior to achieve desired results*—for example, to consider a medical intervention or to change a lifestyle habit. How much easier will each

> *Trust is the gold of interpersonal influence.*

leadership event be if the patient already has high regard for you and an eagerness to work with you? Or even more importantly, an implicit trust in you? Trust is the gold of interpersonal influence.

The "How" of Leading Another

Influencing another individual is obviously a complex endeavor and one that certainly merits more focus and training in physicians' careers. Leading another requires sharpening the tools in your interpersonal toolset. And by far the most important of these tools is a collection of skills and practices that can be grouped under the heading, "active listening." Active listening is the master skill of one-on-one leadership. Though this book is not a granular "how to," let's delve into active listening just a bit, because of its importance.

Active listening

Listening is the foundation of leading. This may sound like an odd assertion to some. Listening, after all, seems inherently passive. When we picture leaders, many of us conjure images of people like General George Patton, Martin Luther King, Jr., or President Ronald Reagan—visionary, magnetic personalities who are able to mobilize masses to action. And while charisma certainly *can* be an aspect of leadership, most day-to-day leaders are much less about the exuberant side of leading and much more about the service side. They know their chief role is to empower people to do *their* best work and to feel fulfilled in what they do. And listening is the way they achieve this—specifically, active listening.

What is *active* listening? Definitions vary, but let's keep ours simple and say that active listening is the art of being fully present to, and fully engaged with, the person who is with you.

President Bill Clinton was a known master of this art. I experienced this once myself when finishing a round of golf at the Army Navy Country Club. I spotted the then-current president at the first tee, ready to start his game. Under the gaze of his Secret Service detail, I introduced myself. He turned his whole body to face me and made full eye contact, his golf game forgotten for the moment, and we chatted a bit—"How was your round? You'll probably beat *me*," that kind of thing. Then he autographed my scorecard, hit his drive, and was on his way. But for those sixty or ninety seconds, l felt like the most important person in his world.

And that's really the goal of active listening: make the other person feel like the center of your world, not a distraction interrupting your day.

There are several components to active listening.

Set the stage

The very first step of active listening is to optimize the physical environment, to the extent possible. Minimize distractions. Close the door. Turn down any ambient music or sound. Close your laptop and shut off your phone—or at least set it aside. Make sure there are no obstructions between you and the other person. If possible, arrange not to be disturbed. If an urgent email needs to be sent, do it first, quickly, so your attention won't be split. The idea is to clear your slate so you can give the conversation your full focus and so the other person will know they are the center of your attention.

Of course, it isn't always possible to alter the environment. Sometimes a coworker grabs you in the hall and wants to talk. If you're under time pressure, let the person know. Say something like, "I really want to hear what you're saying but I only have a few minutes right now. If we need more time, we can set something up for later." And then give the person your full attention for the thirty seconds you do have. People are forgiving of physicians and their busy schedules, but you need to explain your time limits rather than give people impatient attention.

Good posture and eye contact

Face the other person fully. Turn your body away from your desk or computer monitor. Put the pen down. Adopt an open and "relaxed but alert" posture. A closed posture suggests lack of receptivity. Folded arms tend to indicate defensiveness.

Make full eye contact, but not in a constant, uninterrupted way. Eye contact is a balancing act. If you don't make enough of it, the person will feel disconnected from you. If you make too much, the person may feel uncomfortable.

Listen with your whole self

Be fully present to the conversation. Don't multitask. Try to turn off any internal conversations that may be playing in your mind. Active listening employs more than the ears; it involves the whole self. You are "listening" with your full slate of faculties—your eyes, your heart, your nervous system, your "gut"—and trying to take in *everything* the other person is saying (or not saying). That person should be your whole world right now. When you give your full self, it is obvious and clearly felt. It is equally obvious when you're preoccupied with other things.

Give active feedback

As the person is speaking, give occasional active responses—nods, smiles, small verbal cues—to show you're with them and to encourage them to go on. No need to overdo it, and don't let your active responses rise to the level of interruption. It is tempting, when listening to someone, to jump in and say things like, "That reminds me of a time when…." This is fine during a casual two-way conversation between friends, but when you're in a listening situation, avoid derailing the other person's train with your own agenda.

Clarify

One very good reason for interrupting is for clarification purposes. If you're not completely clear on what the person is saying, ask clarifying questions. The person will not see this as an intrusion, but rather as a sign of interest. You care enough about what they're saying that you want to be sure you get it right.

Engage beyond the words

Only a minor percentage of the meaning of any communication is carried by the actual words; the majority is conveyed by body language, tone of voice, facial expressions, and other nontextual indicators. As a demonstration of this, read a page of a screenplay and then watch the same scene played out by actors in a movie. The actor provides layers of emotion, intention, and meaning that words on a page can't possibly capture. Or think about text messaging. Have you ever been offended or alarmed by a text only to find out later that the writer's intentions were completely different from what you thought?

Minding the nontextual cues, both sent (by you) and received (by the other), is a huge part of active listening. Be aware of your own expressions, postures, and gestures—and the messages you're sending with them—and also pay attention to those of the other person. A hesitance in the voice, a smile that seems forced, or a failure to make eye contact can signal that the person has not said all they need to say. You can and should explore this. You might, for example, say, "You don't seem completely comfortable with that. Is there something more?"

Listen to understand

Your entire goal, when active listening, is to understand what the other person is saying and feeling. *Your* agenda must be left outside the door, for now. If you're thinking about the next thing you want to say, you're not really listening. Similarly, if you are mentally defending yourself, crafting an opinion, or thinking about the advice you plan to offer, you are not trying to understand the other person. For now, that's your only job—to understand. The time for advising or commenting will (or may not need to) come later.

A good listener's intention is not simply to comprehend *data* but to understand the other person's *feelings and attitudes* toward the subject, as well as the reason they wanted to talk about it. If the person wanted to impart information only, they would have sent an email. In most cases, when people want to talk, it's because they have feelings about the subject they want to express or explore. It's your job, as the leader and active listener, to find out what those feelings are.

Reflect back

At intervals in the conversation, reflect the person's message back to them in your own words, so they know you are following them. You can do this with phrases like, "In other words…" or "What I'm hearing you say is…."

It's also important to *emotionally* reflect what the other person is conveying. If they're telling you a funny story, smile and laugh in response; if they're sharing something difficult, adopt a sober attitude. *Mirroring* is a term for emulating the verbal tone and body language of another person in conversation. It's something we do unconsciously all the time, and it works to build rapport.

At the end of conversations, sum up what you believe you heard the person say, giving them an opportunity to correct or refine your understanding.

Ask open-ended questions

A great way to ensure you're doing more listening than talking is to ask open-ended questions. These are questions that can't be given one-word answers and are designed to encourage the other person to expand. Open-ended questions often start with phrases such as, "How do you feel about [x]?", "What has your experience been with [y]?", or "What's your take on [z]?"

Silence is gold

Silence is fine from time to time. In fact, as any police detective or psychotherapist knows, silence can be a powerful conversation-shifter. When you allow deliberate silences, the other party tends to want to fill them. When they do so, they often shift to new levels of honesty. As I was writing this chapter, a famous murder trial was concluding, and the defendant was found guilty. The prosecutor, explaining his strategy, said that he remained deliberately silent at frequent intervals when the accused was on the witness stand. The defendant would then start rambling and essentially "trap himself." While we certainly don't want our conversational partners to trap themselves, we do want them to open up.

Active listening is something you can practice every day, at every opportunity.

Building relationships

To influence another human being, especially over a prolonged period, it is best to develop a meaningful relationship with them. Relationships are built on the two core elements discussed earlier—trust and caring. People must know you care about them and that they can trust you. You certainly can't be best friends with everyone in your sphere of influence, but the more trustworthy and caring you are, the better you are able to influence the individuals around you.

The key to developing trust is to behave with integrity with each member of your team and with your patients. Do what you promise them and try to live your values and principles. The caring aspect stems from simply taking the time, on a regular basis, to find out how people are doing and to offer help if needed. It also flows from appreciating team members for who they are and what they bring to the team. There is an old saying, "The gods ask little but that they be remembered," and perhaps that can be said of all of us. We all want to be seen for who we are and what we contribute.

When it comes to relationships with team members, you can decide how personal you want those relationships to be. There is no right or wrong answer. Some of us are comfortable having friendly, family-like relationships with coworkers in which everyone knows one another's cookie recipes; others are not. To use another former president as an example, George H. W. Bush was known for his uncanny ability to remember the life details of the people he met, a trait that endeared him to many. But whether you choose to have familiar relationships or maintain some professional distance, your relationships must have the quality of genuineness.

When cultivating one-on-one relationships, psychological size again comes into play. The title "Doctor" carries a status differential that must be accounted for. People tend to put physicians on pedestals to some extent, whether we like it or not. But of course, it's hard to have a relationship with a person on a pedestal. That's why I, personally, downplay my title and try to get colleagues and coworkers to call me by my first name and treat me as a peer. I'm largely unsuccessful at this, but I'm genuine in my attempts.

Even if you believe your coworkers think of you as "one of the guys/gals," that probably isn't the case. There's a gap you can't just wish away. You need to address it with a sustained and demonstrated openness to others' feedback and a willingness (and ability) to talk to people as peers. That includes a sensitivity to their culture, their personality, their background, their age, their belief systems, their interests, and more.

A true measure of leadership is the way your team members act when you're not present. Do they carry on in your spirit and style, or is there a noticeable change? Much of the answer to that will flow from the relationships you have built, one at a time.

Positive focus

One of the most powerful ways to influence people, one at a time, is to focus on their positive traits and what they do well. Everyone wants to be recognized for their strengths and talents, not merely corrected on what they're doing wrong. When we shine light on people's best traits, those traits tend to grow larger and larger, like plants in the sun.

The classic *Les Misérables* features one of the most moving scenes in literature. Jean Valjean,

> *When we shine light on people's best traits, those traits tend to grow larger and larger, like plants in the sun.*

an escaped convict, is given shelter for the night in a rectory. He steals some silverware and is caught by the police. When his host, a bishop, has the chance to condemn him, he instead tells the police the silver was a gift and proceeds to give Valjean a pair of silver candlesticks to go with the stolen silver. Valjean is confused and overwhelmed by the gesture. The bishop, in his compassion and wisdom, has chosen to recognize the inherent virtue in Valjean rather than call him out for his sins. Valjean rises to the gesture, turns his life around, and uses the silver to build a business and become an honest and compassionate employer.

When leading other individuals, you can play to their "angels" or their "devils." By assuming the best intentions in people, you tend to *bring out* those best intentions. Similarly, if you take the time, often, to praise their strengths and talents, they will bring more and more of those strengths to the table. But if you only correct their errors, they will bring feelings of self-doubt and tentativeness to the table.

It may sound like stating the obvious, but a strong team is built on strength. You forge that strength, one person at a time, by spending most of your time focusing on positive traits and only a small amount of time correcting "flaws." People want to follow those who bring out the best in them.

Influencing Specific Individuals

Physicians have a variety of one-on-one encounters each day, most of which can be thought of as leadership events, and each of which carries its own considerations.

Patients and family members

When dealing with patients and their families, it's helpful to put yourself in their shoes. Virtually no one *wants* to see a doctor. The fact that a patient is in your office usually means they're already having a bad day. They're in pain or they're worried about their health. We are so used to our routines that we can lose sight of the fact that simply taking a blood pressure reading may be highly stress-inducing to the patient. If they're getting an x-ray to learn if their cancer is back or lab tests to see if their kidney is failing, that stress multiplies tenfold. And, of course, if they've been injured or are having a heart attack, they're already in full-blown crisis.

Consider assuming the worst as you walk into a patient room. Assume the patient is fearful or anxious and that you will need to help them through it. If they're fine, they will tell you, and you can ease off. Also, assume the patient wants to be an active participant in their own healthcare, and engage with them on that level. The paternalistic, doctor-knows-best attitude no longer flies as a default position. Today's patients can be distrustful of medicine. They need to trust you before trying even a routine intervention. But even in cases where they *prefer* the old-fashioned, paternalistic approach, you always have an opportunity to get them to assume more ownership of their health.

When interacting with patients, give them your full attention. Don't stare at your laptop or monitor, taking notes. A couple of minutes of your uninterrupted attention will work wonders for patient relationships. Encounters feel longer when attention is full and undivided. Patients need to believe you're going to do your best for them, and that kind of trust is difficult to develop if your face is glued to a computer screen.

Families need that belief too. That message was driven home for me even as I was working on this chapter. A six-year-old boy was going in for emergency brain surgery, and I was meeting with the parents beforehand. I had a hundred things on my mind and was mentally preparing to do the surgery. But the parents wanted to talk about their son, and, of course, I wanted to let them. They showed me a picture of him when he was healthy so I would know the person I was operating on, and I assured them they would have their smiling boy back in no time. Taking just those two minutes to share that photo with me gave those parents the faith to put their trust in me, and by that afternoon, their son was laughing and eating pizza. The parents were extremely grateful, perhaps as much for the time I spent with them as for the surgery itself.

Cultural competence is another important aspect of leading patients (and team members). This involves speaking in clear language the patient can understand and being sensitive to the references and idioms you use. It also means being fully respectful of a patient's beliefs, religion, values, and behaviors, and recognizing that people with different cultural and socioeconomic backgrounds may have different perceptions and expectations of healthcare. It's helpful to learn about the various cultures you regularly serve in your practice while still individualizing interactions. Our patients are members of a culture but also individuals. Take cues from their behaviors and practice empathy as the bottom line.

Team members

In addition to the earlier points about influencing team members, try to be mindful of the fact that your coworkers bring their whole selves to work, and they may have their own health issues. Just because someone is a doctor or a nurse or a technician doesn't mean they can't have cancer, heart disease, or diabetes. So, if you're making comments, as a medical leader, about how patients should take better care of themselves, be careful you're not insulting, discouraging, or frightening your team members unintentionally.

On a separate note, when dealing with team members remember that although you may be their leader on one level, most of them have other bosses. Your authority as a physician derives from writing orders and making medical decisions. But healthcare is a matrixed organization, and almost all your teammates report to someone else as their direct supervisor. Conflicting agendas may exist. Yours might be all about spending time with each patient to make them feel comfortable; their boss's might be all about throughput. It's important to recognize those dual lines of authority, and if your teammates seem to be consistently struggling to meet your preferences, maybe it's because they're responding to conflicting directives. In that case, you may want to speak with their boss to mitigate this type of conflict.

Peers

There are a few things to keep in mind when trying to influence fellow doctors. One is that you can't assume your peers necessarily view you as a peer. Here again, psychological size can factor in. If you're a senior physician with graying temples and years of experience, your "peers" may give you a level of deference you're not necessarily seeking. Conversely, if you're the "new kid on the block," your opinion may be taken with a heftier grain of salt.

When trying to influence medical peers, remember that as doctors we are culturally conditioned to be strong, autonomous figures with a lot of authority. And so, we typically need to be well convinced before trying something new. That's not necessarily a bad thing, and medical peers can be a great resource. If you're trying to initiate change in your organization, it's a great idea to go to the doctors early on, because they will ask tough questions and poke holes in your plans. That can be a terrific aid in refining your strategy. Also, collecting allies in your push for change is a smart idea, and like everything we have been discussing so far, that happens one doctor at a time.

Medical students and residents

When influencing doctors-in-training, try to model the kind of respect you want them to give their peers and patients. In my opinion, however, it's equally important not to coddle them. Medicine is a stressful profession. Making residents uncomfortable isn't necessarily a bad thing. Why? They are entering a profession that entails life-and-death decision-making, and you need to build them up to that. Putting them on the spot occasionally when they don't have an answer or they've made a technical error is a way of reminding them, "What will you do when you're on the big stage and this situation occurs?"

Finding teachable moments throughout the day is vital too, not only to correct errors but to reinforce leadership strengths. It's on us, as working doctors, to help change the culture of medical education by coaching residents as *they* attempt to *influence thoughts and behavior to achieve results*. If you see them doing something correctly from a leadership perspective, commend them on it. The first few times you do this, they may be surprised. Their attitude might be, *Where is this coming from? I thought you were supposed to be teaching me neurosurgery.* But in the leadership-focused culture I am proposing we develop here, our job should also be to teach them how to lead.

Bosses

An aspect of leadership is to "lead up," to try *to influence the thought and behavior* of those above you on the organizational chart. You do this in the ways we have discussed—by having good communication skills, asking questions, building trust, and acting with integrity. You also do it by knowing the parameters of your role. Citing the military again, I recall reading in my first copy of *The Army Officer's Guide*—it's been a while so I'm paraphrasing heavily here—*your responsibility as a junior officer is to present to your commander an analysis of the plan from your perspective, along with any recommended changes. And then, once the decision is made, even if it opposes all your recommendations, to execute that plan as if it were your own.*

It's important, when dealing with bosses, to make sure they know *you* see your role this way. Although you might argue passionately for a given course of action, you are ultimately all in with whatever decision is made. If they don't know you have this attitude, they might interpret your attempts to sway them as opposition. However, knowing you intend to faithfully execute their plan in the end, they will usually (not always) be grateful for your honest input, advice, and perspective. So, it's important to be explicit about this from the beginning.

And now let's look at how influencing individuals leads to an ability to lead teams.

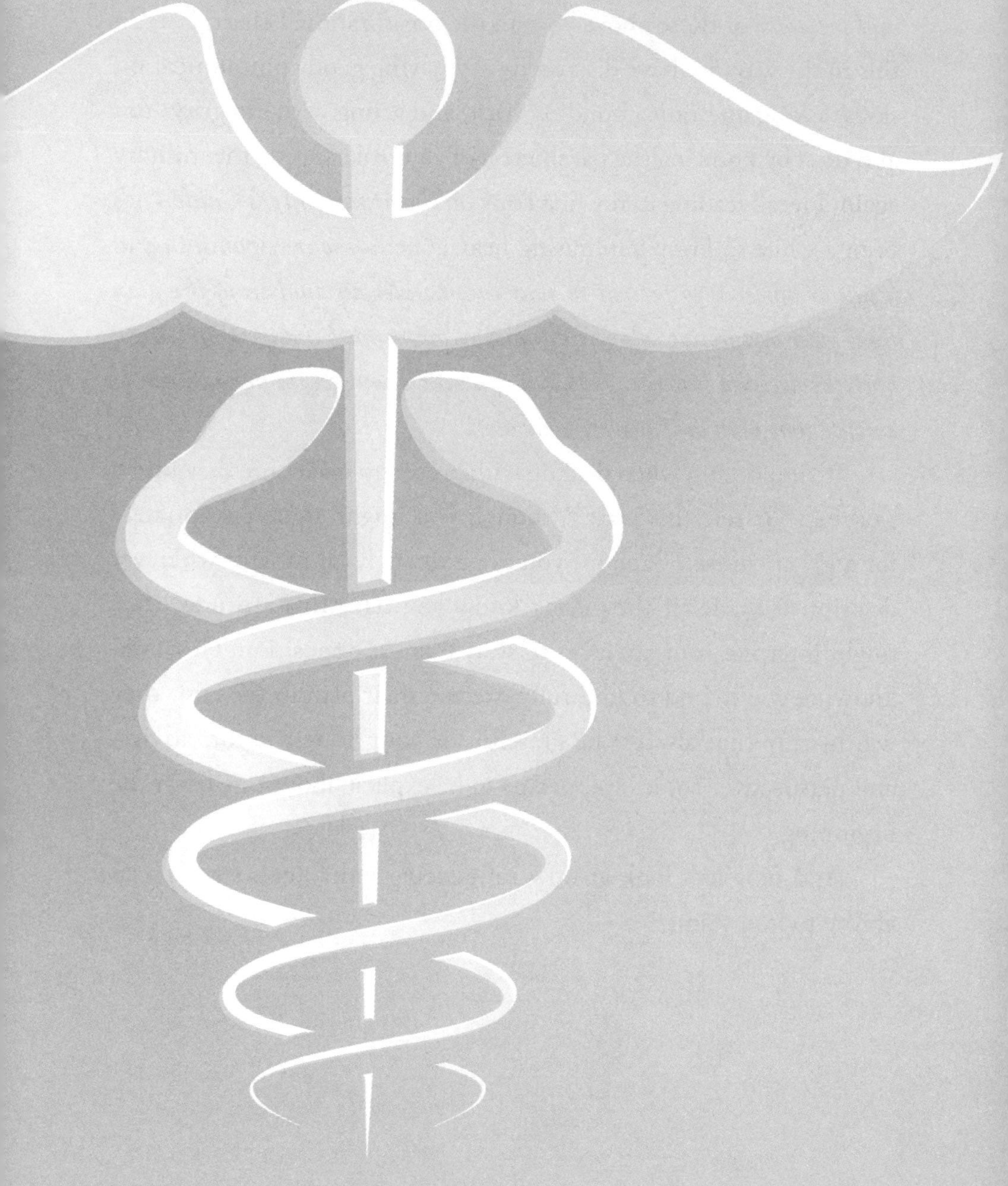

CHAPTER 6

Leadership Circle #3:

Leading Teams

*People buy into the leader
before they buy into the vision.*

- JOHN MAXWELL

Leadership Scenario 1

A patient is scheduled for 7:30 a.m. surgery. The prep work has been delayed a bit, and because of the complexity of the surgery, the anesthesiologist requires extra time to set up the drugs and devices that will keep the patient sedated throughout the long procedure. The surgeon, eager to get started, pokes her head into the OR at 8:45 and sees the anesthesiologist still at work. Knowing it is no longer permissible to "drop the f-bomb" in the OR, she makes her displeasure known by looking at her watch and shaking her head, making sure the anesthesiologist sees her. As she's backing out of the room, she mutters to the rest of the team, "Great, another anesthesia delay."

Leadership Scenario 2

The same story—the anesthesiologist requires more time setting up the drugs for this complex procedure. The surgeon pokes her head into the OR, and the anesthesiologist gives her a slightly apologetic glance. The surgeon, making sure the rest of the team hears her, says, "No worries. Take your time. My rule is I don't rush you; you don't rush me. That's what's best for the patient." The surgeon leaves the room, and the anesthesiologist says, "I wish everyone felt like that."

After leading yourself and leading other individuals, the next outward ring in the circles of leadership is leading teams. It's at the team leadership level where your leadership capability really shines and where you exercise many of the skills we typically attribute to leaders. It is also here where your gaps in leadership reveal themselves for all to see.

"Graduating" to Leading Teams

As I've said before, there is a pattern in medicine (and other fields) whereby those who bring value to the organization are rewarded by being promoted to higher levels of leadership. That value may be a reflection of their clinical skills, prominence as an author or researcher, or revenue generation. This may result in them being promoted from a skill area where they have a high degree of competence to an area where they don't. There can be a good rationale for this—for instance, when the organization is actively developing a person's leadership potential—but we should take care not to use promotions to formal leadership positions as a carrot without preparing people for it. Clinical skills are vitally important in medicine, no question about it, but leadership skills also influence patient experience and outcomes. Clinical skill is necessary but not sufficient to ensure good medical leadership. Leaders must be able to *influence thought and behavior to achieve desired results.*

This brings us back to the premise of the book. By building leadership training into the curriculum of every physician training program we establish a pool of doctors who are ready for team leadership when it is thrust upon them. We also create a means of identifying those who may *not* be gifted at organizational leadership and whose clinical, research, or teaching achievements should perhaps be rewarded in other ways.

Leading teams in healthcare can be extraordinarily rewarding. Here is where you get to see, in real time, the difference your leadership skills can make. A high-performing team—the product of good leadership—has a dynamism and flow that is unmistakable, and its effect on patient care is something you can feel, every day.

Team leadership is a natural progression from the first two circles of leadership. It is important to develop excellent self-awareness and self-discipline (Circle 1). This enables you to have a positive and sustainable influence on individuals, such as patients and team members (Circle 2). Your ability to lead individuals gives you the skills to lead multiple individuals (Circle 3)—because, as I have said many times, leading teams *is* leading individuals.

But leading teams layers more complexity on top of simply leading their component members.

Groups Have a Life of Their Own

As a team leader, you not only need to have effective one-on-one interactions with each member of the group, but you also need to lead them *as* a group.

As soon as you have more than two people in a room, things become complicated. Teammates begin interacting with one another as well as with you. And you don't control all those interactions. Some people may be fully in sync with you and your mission. Some may have their own agendas and may be trying to influence others in a different direction.

And remember, team members also interact when you're not in the room. You might have a meeting with the group, and you might think it went beautifully, but as soon as it's over, people will talk among themselves about what you just said. There may be some in the group who reinforce your message. There may be others who detract from it and are trying to win people into their "camp." And all of this will happen out of your sight and your control.

Part of group leadership is developing a sensitivity to whether everyone is rowing in the same direction—here, in this moment, and on an overall basis—and to reset the cadence if they're not.

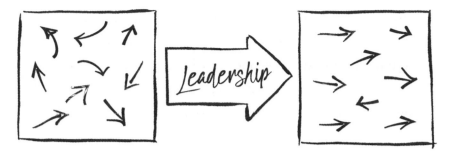

The graphic above shows the leader's effect on getting (most of) the team to align with the mission. When I draw this during lectures, I remind folks of the scene near the end of "Finding Nemo" when Dory gets all the fish in the net to swim down and free themselves—a great leadership visual.

Addressing the team as a group

The skills of active listening are vitally important when leading your team as a group.

Addressing a group is a dynamic event, where you need to be in "receiving mode" as much as in "sending mode." That means in addition to thinking about the message you're delivering, you need to be reading the signals the team is sending you. People often behave a bit differently when in a group than they do when you meet with them one-on-one. They may feel freer to yawn, look at their cellphones, fold their arms unreceptively, whisper to each other, and so on. Their behavior can often be more revealing in group settings. Try to use this to your advantage. Adopt an active listening mindset and try to read what people's behavior is telling you.

Who is leaning forward in their seat, holding eye contact with you, and smiling and nodding in an enthused way? Whose eyes are glazed over and is not participating? Are there team members whose folded arms and raised eyebrows tell you they aren't buying into what you're selling? Who appears to be understanding your message and who doesn't?

In every group interaction, there are potential leadership opportunities you can seize. Let's say, for instance, a lively discussion is going on, and you see someone who looks like they want to participate but they're shy or they can't get a word in edgewise. Try to give them the floor: "Katie, it looks like you have something to say." Pull them into the conversation. Show, by your leadership, that their perspective is important and valued. And when they offer their thoughts, give them feedback, such as, "Thanks, that's a great point. Did everybody hear that?" This tells the whole team that everyone's input is valued. Over time, when you do this consistently, a sense of psychological safety develops.

I once observed a leader respond to a teammate in a meeting by saying: "John stay in your lane." Needless to say I took that as an opportunity to do some very directed coaching with both individuals, and the team. I made sure John knew to speak up even in discussions outside his professional expertise. In private later I quite pointedly let the leader know why we value everyone's input and how the statement prevented the open discussion we need to make the best decisions—and frankly made it clear that I never wanted to hear that phrase again. I also addressed the team later to reinforce the message that all ideas were welcome.

Try to treat every sign of boredom, resistance, or opposition as an opening. Anyone who is not buying your message probably has an opinion that varies from yours. You want to find out what that opinion is. You want to tap into the intelligence of the whole group to make sure your ideas are being fully vetted and explored from all angles.

Addressing team members separately

It's not always wise or appropriate to try to draw people out in front of the group. You can take them aside later. "You seemed like you had something more to say. What are your thoughts on this?" And really try to pull it out of them, even if they're uncommunicative. It may take a few tries, as there may be deeper issues at play. Maybe the person was supposed to get your job and they're resentful about that. Maybe there's something going on at home and they're preoccupied. Paying attention to the cues and following up is crucial.

An understanding of group dynamics is helpful, and it's wise to read a book or two on the topic.[15] Know that there are both official and unofficial leaders in every team, and that some of these people, especially if they've been around for a while, can have tremendous influence on other team members. It's important to get them on your side and make sure they understand your goals and support those goals within the team when you're not around.

If you see one of these unofficial leaders acting enthusiastic and supportive about one of your initiatives, build on that. Tell them *you're* excited they're on board. Ask how you can help them move the agenda forward. Find out what resources they need.

If, on the other hand, an informal leader seems to be resistant to the plan, try speaking to them offline. That can be difficult, of course, but you need to assume they want the same things you want—excellent patient care, efficient teamwork, a good atmosphere. But something isn't working for them. And you need to find out what that is.

A less confrontational way I've found to get people talking is to ask them, "What's worrying you about *x*?" There's nothing accusatory

---

15   Maxwell, *17 Laws of Teams*; Covey, *Speed of Trust*; Sinek, *Leaders Eat Last*.

about that question. It shows you're interested in their perspective, and it gives them a platform to share their concerns.

If you can get someone who habitually disagrees with you to see that you're both on the same team and to trust you, that person can become a powerful ally. They probably have a perspective you need to hear. Several times, over the course of my career, I have deliberately promoted people who have been a bit of a thorn in my side. Baffled colleagues will come to me and say, "Why did you put Susan in charge of [x]? She's always challenging you." And I'll reply, "That's why I promoted her. I value both her perspective and her willingness to share it."

Leadership Styles Matter

As you "graduate" to leading groups (and even when you're leading people one-on-one), it is important to recognize that there are many styles of leadership. Different styles are effective in different situations. It helps to be self-aware (here's Circle 1 again) about the style you are using at any given time. Leaders who lack self-awareness often remain locked in one or two leadership styles without even realizing there are other options. Skilled, self-aware leaders choose their leadership style based on the needs of the situation and with a long-term vision in mind as to how those choices impact the team's performance over time.

Much has been written about leadership styles. Various authors have broken these down into as few as three types (authoritative, democratic, and laissez-faire) and as many as eleven. It's not particularly important which school of categorization you adopt, but it is important to recognize that you do have options in your leadership approach. Once again, if you are unaware of which style you are using and how it fits the situation, you likely aren't optimizing your leadership performance. A good breakdown of leadership styles is the one used by Daniel Goleman, Richard Boyatzis, and Annie McKee in *The New Leaders: Transforming the Art of Leadership into the Science of Results.*

- *Commanding*—The leader makes all the decisions and essentially gives orders, telling everyone what to do.

- *Pacesetting*—The leader emphasizes excellence and leads by example, setting the pace for the rest of the team and expecting them to match it.

- *Visionary*—Team members are invited to buy into the leader's long-term vision and behave in ways consistent with achieving that vision. Inspiration is crucial in this style.

- *Democratic*—A participatory form of leadership in which all team members have a say in the decision-making process, although the leader makes the final decision.

- *Affiliative*—A style of leadership based on relationships. The leader focuses on creating a positive work environment, mainly by using praise and rewards rather than negative feedback.

- *Coaching*—The leader takes a developmental approach, trying to help team members improve as professionals and as human beings. A focus is on building future leaders.[16]

There are several other styles, such as laissez-faire, in which the leader takes a hands-off approach and steps in only as needed; *transactional*, where the main focus is on rewarding team members based on what they contribute to the organization; *bureaucratic*, which is a "by the books"

---

16   Goleman, D., Boyatzis, R. E., & McKee, A. (2002). The new leaders: Transforming the art of leadership into the science of results.

approach; and *leader as servant,* whereby the leader focuses on the needs of the team members and how to give them what they need.

All these forms of leadership have their place, and seasoned leaders learn to instinctually shift from one to another as the situation demands and often to use multiple styles at once.

In general, the last four in the Goleman list are the emotionally positive ones and the ones you want to chiefly rely on when building a high-performance healthcare team. The commanding and pacesetting styles should be used only sparingly. Of course, there are times—for example, in the trauma bay or during a code in the ICU—when a commanding or pacesetting style may be optimal. But even in these cases, your team will be more responsive to you if you have been using more democratic, affiliative, and coaching approaches the rest of the time.

Unfortunately, in medicine, the opposite often happens. We physicians tend to rely on the commanding and pacesetting styles because that's consistent with the pace we've held through college, medical school, residency, fellowship, and our daily job. As doctors, we are extremely busy and under constant stress. We never have enough time to get everything done, so it's natural to stay in the pacesetting mode and try to transmit that energy to everyone around us. The commanding style also comes naturally, because a "captain of the ship" mentality is taught early in medical school and reinforced continually thereafter. For example, we are all familiar with the classic morbidity and mortality ("M&M") conferences following undesirable patient outcomes. Every decision made by the whole team is hyper-analyzed, but most often the attending physician is considered responsible as the ultimate decision-maker and captain of the ship.

The commanding and pacesetting styles, which many physicians use almost exclusively, are the least effective with teams over time. These leader-centric styles do little to promote trust and psychological safety. They do not build self-confidence and leadership skills in team members. And they can exclude valuable team insights that would help improve patient care. Physicians would do well to broaden their palette of leadership styles if they wish to promote high performance over the long term.

Most of the time, on most days, it is vastly preferable to use a mix of the more positive, "other"-focused styles. Seek your team's input on plans (democratic), try to build positive, caring relationships (affiliative), teach your team members whenever the opportunity presents itself (coaching), and don't be afraid to inspire people (visionary).

Self-Awareness and Authenticity in Team Leadership

Managing your leadership styles requires self-awareness. This includes making conscious choices in the way you present yourself to team members (and patients). There is a lot of talk these days about "bringing your authentic self to work," and this is important, especially if you want to build relationships with your team. You want to be seen as a full and genuine human being, not as a cardboard caricature of a "doctor." We've looked at examples of how beneficial it can be to share yourself honestly with your team.

At the same time, a balance must be struck. It's equally important to present a positive, capable image to the organization and to the people you're leading. There can sometimes be a tension between being your authentic self and being what your organization, team, patients, and families need you to be on a given day. If you're having personal issues or you're not at your best physically, sometimes it's better to put on a "stiff upper lip" and soldier on. Again, it's all about balance. Too much personal transparency can weaken your team leadership, as can too much opacity.

And remember, your position as a doctor carries psychological size you can't erase simply by acting like "one of the guys/gals." For example, you might be tempted to engage in playful banter with your teammates, where everyone makes fun of each other, but remember: your remarks carry more weight and can cause more pain than those of others (remember the earlier quoted advice that "self-deprecating humor is the only kind commanders can afford"). The power differential your position affords you must also be carefully considered when inviting personal relationships with team members.

Leadership Principles and Practices for High-Performing Teams

The highest purpose of leadership in medicine is to improve patient care by fostering high performance in our teams. As noted earlier, high-performing teams have distinctive qualities you can see and feel. Teammates genuinely care for one another and for patients. They know each other's rhythms and strengths, and they rely on them. You never hear anyone saying, "That's not my job"—rather, people pitch in where they're needed and go the extra mile and the extra hour. Teammates would "take a bullet" for one another, even those they may not consider friends.

Creating high-performing teams requires leadership. And it requires using a range of skills you learn only by practicing a variety of leadership styles. Here are some principles and practices I have seen work well over many years of serving as a physician leader at various levels:

Let the team drive the bus

If I had to distill everything I've learned about leadership down to one sentence, it would be a version of the advice Jim Collins gives in his book *Good to Great*: Get the right people on the bus and put them in the right seats. In addition, good leaders should give them the right resources, give them a sense of direction, and get out of the way. Breaking that down into its component parts:

- *Get the right people on the bus*—hire great people with great skills: people who share your vision for high performance and patient care.

- *Put them in the right seats*—give people the job and set of responsibilities that leverage their strengths and talents most fully. Don't "promote" them from jobs they're great at to jobs they're not well-suited for. Find other ways to reward them.

- *Give them the right resources*—continually ask your people, "Do you have what you need?" and strive to give them what they require, even if you must fight for it.

- *Give them a sense of direction*—clearly and repeatedly communicate your vision and work with them to create goals to strive for.

- *Get out of their way*—don't micromanage or play Master and Commander (unless the situation dictates). You have put these great people on your team for a reason. Let them do what they do best.

Leave no one behind

The military has a precept whereby you don't abandon a fallen comrade. You never say, "Someone's lost out there, but we won't send four people to go find them, because then we'll be risking four more lives." No, you send *eight* people to go find them. Why? Because you want everyone to know that if *they're* lost out there, you'll come for them too. During the COVID crisis, many team members fell sick, and it was vitally important that we gave them excellent care—not only because they fully deserved it but also to show others who were risking their lives how we would treat *them* if they got sick.

This principle applies in the little things too. If you see someone having a tough day, buy them a cup of coffee. If someone's voice isn't being heard, draw out their perspective and share it with the team. If someone's contributions are being taken for granted, give them special recognition. This tells the team you're paying attention to everyone. "Leave no one behind" means no one is forgotten; every teammate is cared for.

Catch people doing well

There is a strange custom in most organizations to give the bulk of management attention to fixing things that are broken, while taking for granted what people are doing well. An 80/20 ratio often persists, whereby 80 percent of management focus goes to correcting errors and weaknesses, while 20 percent (at most) goes to praising people for doing things right. Try flipping that ratio around. Spend 80 percent, or more, of your time and energy "catching people doing right," and only 20 percent, or less, addressing weaknesses.

For example, when you see a team member disinfecting a patient room, stop and say something like, "I love how clean you keep this place. If I was a patient, I'd feel safe and welcome here. Thank you." Take special care to praise any behaviors you are trying to increase— for example, people stepping in and doing whatever jobs need to be done. Constantly remind teammates that they are indeed helping with patient care, even if they don't directly interact with patients.

It is a simple fact that whatever we feed with attention increases. Calling attention to people's strengths increases those strengths. It also creates a positive moment that feels good to you and to the person you are praising. It's a win/win/win. I will never understand why this isn't more obvious to all managers and leaders.

Heartfelt and genuine thank-yous, given out frequently, can accomplish more to sustain morale than most sophisticated (and expensive) management programs.

Encourage debate

Team members can and should disagree. You want to hear everyone's opinion, to ensure all decisions are as well-considered as possible. In high-performance teams, people *debate*, but they don't *fight*. That is, they don't take disagreements personally. Your team must regard the offering of critical feedback as a professional duty, not as a personal affront. This requires team members to check their egos at the door and actively seek differing opinions. Teammates should come to meetings seeking the best decision rather than defending a position. The quote, "We debate not to win, but to discover truth," should be embraced.

> *In high-performance teams, people **debate**, but they don't **fight**—and they debate not to win, but to discover truth.*

As a leader, you can create a safe environment in which team members can voice their points of view, sometimes passionately, without insulting others or feeling insulted. All ideas should be welcomed and protected, even if they don't end up being used. Invite and welcome feedback about your own behaviors and practices as well. The way you handle personal criticism models the way you want other people to handle feedback.

Some leaders take criticism personally. In extreme cases, when someone disagrees with them, they fire that person or find some other way to get rid of them. In doing so, they likely lose a valuable perspective and certainly inhibit others from speaking up. As leaders, we can't afford the luxury of feeling we are "the smartest person in the room."

A high-performing team is made up of people who trust one another and are united in purpose but who feel safe expressing their point of view, even when it differs from those of teammates.

Care

At the risk of sounding sanctimonious, I believe we are put on this planet to take care of each other. That's why I became a doctor and why I enjoy leading teams. I suspect the same is probably true for you. Therefore, it's crucial that we show genuine concern for the people we are privileged to call teammates. Care is something that can't be faked, but it can be reinforced and communicated—by asking teammates how they're doing and offering support as needed; by recognizing them for what they do; by rewarding them with good pay and benefits (if we control those things); by showing them every day that they matter as human beings, not just as employees. A sense of mutual caring is a hallmark of high-performing teams. And it flows from the leader.

Celebrate victories

High performance should be acknowledged, rewarded, and celebrated. When the team's good work saves a patient who might otherwise have died, for example, that is a victory. Treat it as such. Make sure to attribute the result directly to the team's skills and commitment.

During the height of COVID-19, teams in my healthcare organization discovered treatment methods and adaptations that were rapidly reported to the rest of the world. Our people led the way in several areas of patient treatment. To know we were part of a team that was changing the way the world fought COVID felt terrific, and we celebrated those victories and used them as motivation to show up again the next day.

Achieving victories is what high performance is all about. Celebrating your wins—never becoming blasé about them—helps keep the high performance going.

Leading teams is perhaps the most exciting aspect of physician leadership. Your positive effect is both immediate and long term, and you see it helping to improve and to save lives, which is the greatest privilege any of us can ask for. The skills you learn leading teams shape your ability to lead departments and entire organizations, the final circle of leadership.

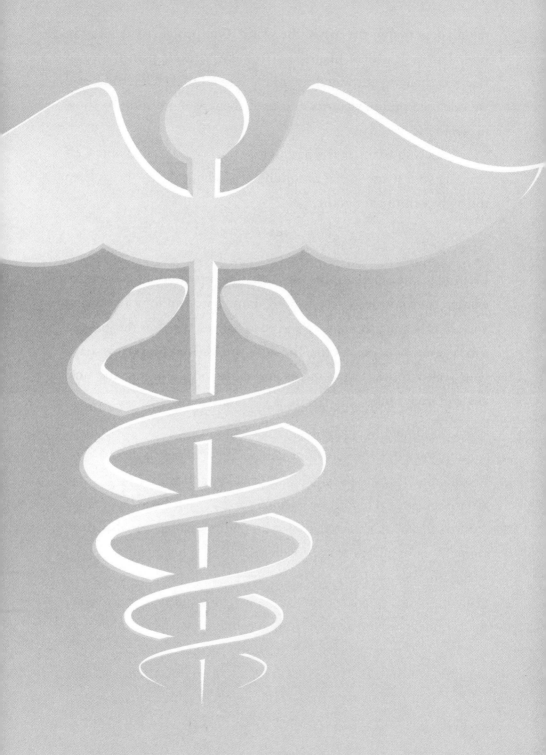

CHAPTER 7

Leadership Circle #4:

Leading Organizations

You manage things; you lead people.

- REAR ADMIRAL GRACE HOPPER

Leadership Scenario

Dr. John Doe is a renowned nephrologist who has had dozens of publications, has generated millions of dollars in grant money, and is very well respected within the hospital where he has worked for the past sixteen years. He leads the relatively small nephrology division, where he has an outstanding reputation with his peers and patients. People follow his lead in committee meetings, and he has always been a compelling leader within that scope. Just recently he was asked by the CEO of the hospital to become the chief medical officer when the current CMO retires this spring. Dr. Doe hasn't given the CEO an answer yet. He is hesitant because he worries that he's just not ready for leadership at that level.

No one is ever ready for the next level up. It *is* a level up, after all—a job you've never done before. When you're considering an opportunity to lead at the organizational level, it can feel like a real sea change. But you need to remind yourself that it's no different from the challenges you've faced in the past. Getting into medical school, your residency training, your first team leadership position.... You gain experience by doing new things; that's the nature of the beast. In any new role it's natural to feel like you're not ready. But it's also good to remind yourself you're not *supposed* to know how to do this yet. You have time to learn.

People *and* Things

As Admiral Hopper's above quote tells us, "You manage things; you lead people." When you get to a senior leadership position within an organization, you will need to do both. And that may be a big change. As a physician you've spent your career leading people—whether you've identified yourself as a leader or not—and now you must add the capacity to manage things. You will now be much more responsible for things like budgets, inventories, and space allocation. You will be involved in strategy and planning and creating emergency response protocols. These are not necessarily skills that are in your toolbelt as a practicing clinician. You will still need to lead, but you'll also need to *manage*.

Fortunately, you won't be doing this alone. In every aspect of running the organization, you will have colleagues who are subject matter experts you can turn to. In addition to the clinical experts you've worked with for years, you will now be surrounded by finance experts, legal experts, logistics experts, quality experts, and more. You should draw from their expertise, both to help you run your new organization and to enhance your education at this next level and beyond. These teammates have spent their careers getting good at things you know relatively little about, and you can learn a lot from their knowledge.

It can be helpful to remind yourself that your role hasn't changed as much as it may seem. You are still trying to *influence thought and behavior to achieve desired results*. You are still leading a team; it's just that the team members have more varied backgrounds and are at higher levels of the organization than your previous team members. And ultimately you will still rely on the main skill you have ideally been working on for years—listening.

A good leader is a good listener, and that doesn't change at the organizational level. In fact, here is where your listening skills become more important than ever. Everyone around you now knows more than you do about their professional domain, and the way you will access that knowledge is by listening—not by talking or by trying to prove your expertise. Humility and a desire to learn are important keys to success at the organizational level.

A Shift in Mindset

The move to organizational leadership requires a shift in mindset that can be rather profound for many physicians. Many of us, when offered higher-level leadership positions, are coming from senior clinician roles. In that domain we are often the "smartest person in the room," so to speak. And now we must shift, in a very real sense, to be being the least smart person in the room. This isn't merely an ego adjustment, it's a whole new way of thinking and working.

Again, this is something I learned first in the military. Imagine, for example, you are an infantry battalion commander. You've spent your entire career in the infantry. First you were an infantry platoon leader, then an infantry company commander, then a staff officer, and now a battalion commander. You know all things infantry better than anyone. You are literally the smartest person in the room when it comes to tactics, operational movement, and combined arms deployment at the infantry battalion level. And when anyone in your battalion wants an answer in these areas, they turn to you.

If a few years later you are promoted to general, you're suddenly leading a division of 15,000 soldiers. Now almost everyone who's briefing you at this level will know more about the subject matter on the slides than you do, whether it is logistics, finance, aviation operations, or healthcare for your soldiers. You've gone from being a tactical leader, filled with expertise, to being a strategic leader who is no longer the smartest person in the room.

No longer just an expert tactician

In the US Military, there is yet another leadership school one attends before consideration for promotion to general or admiral (this school is one full year—another testament to the commitment to leadership development in our armed forces). As we were taught at the Eisenhower School, one of those Senior Service Colleges, when you transition from being a tactical leader—such as a physician—to being a strategic leader, your job shifts from having the right answers to asking the right questions. As Melissa Karz puts it in her article, "The Four Habits of Strategic Leaders," "The tactical mindset is about getting things done, putting out fires and being the expert. The strategic mindset is about aligning with organizational objectives, discovering the unknowns and being a facilitator between ideas, people and plans."[17]

Let's say you're a mid-career physician, and you have fifteen years of experience practicing your specialty. You're much like that battalion commander. You are the expert in most rooms you enter. Gaining expertise is the way you've always thrived, as with most physicians. When you were a medical student, you studied and accumulated knowledge. When you were a resident on rounds and the attending doctor asked a tough question, you went to the literature and came back with the answer. When, as a practicing physician, you met a new patient with a condition you hadn't seen before, you pulled all the articles you could find and learned how experts around the world were dealing with this unusual condition. And you became the smartest person in your hospital about that rare illness.

This process is ingrained in all of us as doctors. *Go out and gain expertise.* But when we are given leadership of an organization, that changes. Suddenly, other people know *far* more than we do. That's the

---

17   Melissa Karz, "Four Habits of Strategic Leaders," Next Step Partners, accessed September 15, 2023, https://nextsteppartners.com/habits-of-strategic-leaders/.

reality. We can't run out and read about, say, organizational finance and then come back a week later knowing more than the CFO. We'll never have enough time to do that—because it would take decades! And so, we need to make the mental switch from tacticians to strategists. We're no longer the person with all the answers. We're the one with the insightful and important questions.

This can be a particularly hard shift for doctors to make—because our drive for expertise is embedded in us and can often be a matter of life and death. And yet, making the shift can also be a tremendous weight off our shoulders. I have practically seen a bulb light up over physicians' heads when they realize, *Hey, I don't have to be smarter than all these people. That's what we're paying* them *for!*

Questioner, not answerer

Your job is now to be a master questioner, to ask the kinds of questions that will send your leadership team probing for solutions. You'll now find yourself thinking about the second- and third-order effects of whatever change is being proposed. *If we do this, what impact will it have on our physician community? On nursing? On patients? On our budget? On how we're perceived by the media? What will the board think? If the plan isn't working, what's our off-ramp? How will we get out of it? When and how do we make that call?* Part of the discipline of asking the right questions is thinking broadly and deeply about what happens if you make this change. What are the consequences? Ask the questions and put the team to work digging for answers.

Multidisciplinary thinking

Whereas formerly you were a vertical thinker, keeping your head down and learning more about your chief discipline, you now must lift your head up, so to speak, and look around in a horizontal way. Not only must you think about how every decision affects every department and discipline, but you must actively seek input from across the organization. You'll want to have your finance team, your HR team, your clinical team, your logistics team, and others in the room whenever a big opportunity is being presented; otherwise, you'll be missing valuable perspectives. Of course, you won't always need or want to have *every* team at the table for every decision, but whenever it's a matter that has broad stakeholder impact, then getting broad stakeholder input is critical. And whenever you're planning major changes, it is essential to put a multidisciplinary team together.

New leadership style needed

Physicians who have relied on the commanding or pacesetting styles of leadership can run into trouble at the organizational level. Giving orders is no longer the most sustainable option. Departmental heads and executives often do not respond well to this kind of communication. The mindset whereby the doctor is the ultimate authority in decision-making must be used sparingly, if at all. Of course if you are the CEO you have that level of responsibility again, but it's wise to be a fair bit more democratic than you may have been used to at the bedside. Skills such as collaborating, iterating on plans, and building consensus become

Humility involves an eagerness to surround yourself with people who know more than you do in almost every area, and to avail yourself of their knowledge.

much more important at this level. Ability to delegate is another skill that is vital for organizational leaders and can be challenging for doctors who are used to working hard and having prime agency.

Humility is more essential than ever when leading at this level. That doesn't imply self-effacement but rather an eagerness to surround yourself with people who know more than you do in almost every area and to avail yourself of their knowledge.

What the Physician Brings to Healthcare Leadership

There has been a long-running discussion in healthcare as to whether physicians make better CEOs of hospitals and healthcare organizations than nonphysicians. Physicians, on the one hand, have expertise in medical service delivery, which, of course, is hospitals' *raison d'être*. On the other hand, physicians tend to have less organizational training than leaders with business-oriented backgrounds. Research results are mixed. Some studies indicate that hospitals employing physician CEOs achieve higher performance scores in several key clinical measures but don't necessarily perform better *financially*. Goodall in 2011 found that on some quality measures a subset of hospitals performed better when physician-led.[18] I coauthored a study in 2020 looking at US acute-care hospitals across several clinical and financial performance measures and found no difference in outcomes with physician CEOs versus nonphysician CEOs.[19]

---

18   Amanda H. Goodall, "Physician-leaders and Hospital Performance: Is There an Association?," *Social Science & Medicine* 73, no. 4 (August 2011): 535–539.

19   Leon Moores, Nancy Borkowski, S. Robert Hernandez, and Amy Yarbrough Landry, "Clinical and Financial Performance of Hospitals with Physician CEOs vs. Nonphysician CEOs," In *Academy of Management Proceedings* (Vol. 2020, No. 1, p. 18131, Briarcliff Manor, NY: Academy of Management, 2020).

The challenge in these and similar studies is the large number of moderating, mediating, and confounding variables between the independent variable CEO characteristic (physician or nonphysician) and the dependent variables measuring system performance. It is difficult to find statistically significant support for a leadership hypothesis when there are hundreds of variables that impact a regression analysis. Cutting through the math, what this implies is that healthcare systems are complex, and humans (leaders) are each so different they cannot be easily categorized into a handful of (or a single) independent variables.

The more important point is this: both physician CEOs and nonphysician CEOs bring important strengths to their senior leadership positions. There is no real "us versus them" debate here. Regardless of who is in the top position, a multidisciplinary leadership team is needed, and nobody can be a subject matter expert in all aspects of running a healthcare organization, including the physician. However, more and more organizations are recognizing that physicians bring a valuable perspective to the upper leadership team.

So as a physician leader, it's important for you to remember why you've been appointed to this position and the lens through which the organization is paying you to see things. And that lens is all about patient outcomes.

As an organizational leader, you need to both broaden your horizons to include many new perspectives *and* continue to bring your patient care perspective robustly to the table. Your ideas won't always win the day. A solution that factors in all perspectives—finance, HR, compliance, IT, and others—will be the best one. You're not there to win a debate. You're there to come up with the best answer for the organization and, therefore, your patients.

For me, that piece of butcher paper always serves as my rudder, even when (*especially* when) I'm leading at higher organizational levels.

I always come back to, "How does this impact patient care and patient outcomes? How does this make us better at our mission?" And I regularly remind myself that my job is simply to *influence thought and behavior toward desired results*. That doesn't mean I get my way in all things, nor should it, but I try to act as a continual gravitational force toward better patient outcomes.

Taking the Reins—Early Priorities

Assuming a major role in organizational leadership is bound to feel a bit overwhelming at first. Writing down your priorities can be helpful. Here are a few things to keep in mind in the early days of your tenure. Other priorities can come later.

Set the tone

One of the first things you do when you take command of a military organization is to take the unit flag from the outgoing commander and hand it back to your senior noncommissioned officer. When he or she then puts the flag into the stand, it starts the clock, symbolizing, "You're in charge now." You then walk straight into your first meeting with your key leaders and you establish your command philosophy and style while also seeking input from your team.

In civilian organizations, you won't be taking "command" per se, but you do want to set the tone of your leadership from the first actions you take. For example, if you give your introductory speech as the new leader and then leave immediately afterward to go have drinks with friends, that says one thing. If you follow your speech by bringing your key leaders together in a "let's get to work" meeting, that says something quite different.

Your first meeting is important, and it matters who you have in the room (notice a theme here?). This is your new leadership team, officially and unofficially. Even if you have been in this organization working with these same people for some time, your role is now different and deserves this critical meeting. Naturally, you will invite key departmental people and subject matter experts to the table, but you also want to think about inviting critical influencers within the organization. Not all these people necessarily have top titles, but if they are able to get things done, you might want them in the room. If this isn't appropriate, you'll want to reach out to them in other ways as soon as possible.

The first meeting with your team allows you to introduce (or reintroduce in your new role) yourself. Remember those priorities we talked about in your Circle 1 self-assessment? Here is your chance to tell your team your priorities, your core values, and your styles. They want to know. This is a stressful time for them, and worry about what the "new boss" is going be like is near the top of the stressor list. Use this meeting to reinforce the sense of mission and the sense of urgency they already have knowing that people's health, welfare, and lives are in your collective hands.

Assess barriers and opportunities

One of the early jobs of a new leader is to assess the organization's barriers and opportunities. This should be done within your first ninety days. There are different models of analysis you can use. A classic business process is the SWOT analysis, by which you analyze your Strengths, Weaknesses, Opportunities, and Threats. This is fairly self-explanatory: You inventory the things you're doing well as an organization and the assets you possess. You take a hard look at the things you need to do better. You analyze the internal and external healthcare landscape to see where opportunities for expansion and improvement exist. You search for internal and external threats to your success and survival.

Chances are, this work has been done at some point before. There's probably a prior SWOT analysis sitting on your shelf or hard drive that you can update. These earlier reports probably contain valuable information, but it's always wise to do your own analysis. You were chosen for this role presumably so you can bring fresh perspectives to the table. Involve your leadership team in the analysis, and let them know it isn't a pro forma exercise, it's meant to form the basis of an action plan.

An excellent book for organizational leaders who are just starting out in their role is Michael D. Watkins's *The First 90 Days: Proven Strategies for Getting Up to Speed Faster and Smarter.*

Assess your own strengths

Along with your analysis of barriers and opportunities, you'll want to do a "personal SWOT analysis" of sorts. Look at the areas where you possess strong knowledge and competence and the areas where you don't. If you've already been leading a department or division, then you may already be familiar with, say, financial data sets or EHR administration, but as CMO or CEO there will be new areas of responsibility beyond your current knowledge base. Ask your team leaders how you can best get up to speed in these areas. These are your "known unknowns."

There are also the "unknown unknowns." One of the big challenges in any new position is that you "don't know what you don't know." You can only fill in gaps you see. For that reason, you might consider earning an advanced degree or certificate in healthcare or business administration. These programs are built by experts in healthcare leadership and management to provide a comprehensive foundation of knowledge. Undoubtedly there will be things in that knowledge set you didn't think of—the unknown unknowns.

Increasing your knowledge is important because, even though you're not going to be the *expert* in most of the subject areas you now oversee, you still need to know enough to have intelligent conversations with your leadership team. You need to be able to ask questions of your finance officer or HR director. You can't afford to be ignorant about any major area of operations or administration.

Assess the culture

A big part of your job when you step into organizational leadership, whether from within or without, is to try to get a read on the culture across the organization. How do people feel about each other? How do they feel about senior leadership, the organization, the community— about all those things that influence how they do their job?

If there is a lot of fear or mistrust of senior leadership, and people feel like they're walking on hot coals, that influences day-to-day behaviors. On the other hand, if the senior leadership is universally adored and there's a warm, family-like feeling about how the organization takes care of its people and the community, that, too, influences people's day-to-day behavior. Staff probably love coming to work and they trust and respect the people they work with. Communication is robust and good decisions are made with great input.

Most of us have had a taste of working for both types of organizations. It's vitally important to get a sense of how people really feel—not the well-crafted mission statement on the lobby wall, but the real feeling.

Changing culture, if necessary, will take a long time, but you need to know where things stand right now. Will you be fighting to repair shattered trust or will you be trying to assure people they won't be losing something treasured? The answers to these questions will color much of what you do from the start.

Ongoing Priorities

As you settle into your role, here are some longer-term priorities to keep in mind.

Communicate the mission

When you land in upper management or organizational leadership, you'll hear a lot of talk about mission and vision. Over the years I have helped craft a lot of mission statements, and it often amazes me how much time and effort people put into wordsmithing the perfect declaration of purpose. I've seen teams of leaders spend many hours in a room agonizing over whether to use the word "enhance" or "improve." But the truth is, if you put two hundred different health-care organizations' mission statements in a hat and pulled one out you could probably mount it on your organization's wall and run with it. In the final analysis, there's not a lot of wiggle room on a healthcare system's mission. Essentially, you're improving the health outcomes of your community, of the patients you're entrusted to care for, and, ultimately, of humanity. The real challenge is not to come up with a mission that's perfectly phrased or differentiates you from "the competition"; it's to find better ways to *accomplish* the mission and to make sure everyone is on board with the simple, but noble, goal they've already signed on for: saving and improving lives.

Here is where it helps to remember that all leadership is a one-on-one event. As a top leader, you have dozens of one-on-one interactions throughout each day with people in your organization. Each of these is an opportunity to reinforce the idea that no matter where your teammates sit in the healthcare system, their jobs are yoked to accomplishment of the mission. When in leadership positions, make it a point to visit with the people in finance, the IT team, and others who never touch a patient and tell them, "We can't do this without you." Say things like, "You keep the electricity on in the OR," or "You put the scalpel in my hand. You are saving lives with the work you do for this organization." Tell people stories of appreciation shown by patients and let them know that they are included in those thanks.

Being a physician gives you added credibility in this. As a doctor, you've been out on the floor, treating patients, and you know exactly how each support system feeds into that work. It's easy for people to forget they're part of a team that's improving health and saving lives; part of your job is to infuse everyone with that sense of mission.

Work patiently on culture

Developing a great culture should be a central goal of every organizational leader. There are hundreds of definitions of culture, but perhaps the simplest way to think of it is just the *feel* of the organization. How do you feel when you walk in? When an employee finishes an eight- or twelve-hour shift, how do they feel? How do people feel about their leaders? Are they walking on eggshells? Are they dreaming of new jobs, or are they deeply invested in the work they're doing and trying to get their friends to join them? That's culture, and it affects every single aspect of how people perform at their jobs. Thus, it affects patient outcomes every day.

If the culture is ailing, it is our job as leaders to cure it, *but* we must recognize that culture changes very, very slowly. A long-term-treatment mindset is needed. It usually takes three to five years, minimum, to get the "patient" responding at all. But to fully cure a bad culture can take a decade or longer. Remember, bad cultures have been infected by years of distrust—people repeatedly being told one thing one month, another the next; people submitting proposals that languish in bureaucratic hell for years; people unable to get the resources they need; people being forced to implement initiatives that make no sense. These things destroy leadership credibility and erode trust. Staff begin to think of leaders as out-of-touch "suits" whose agendas are far removed from patient health. An "us versus them" mentality prevails.

If you're coming into this kind of environment as the senior leader, start from day one assessing the culture and then working to try to repair it. That means building trust by delivering on small promises at first. It means acting with integrity and transparency. It means improving communications by listening to people at every level of the organization. It means actively soliciting hard criticism and then instituting changes based on that feedback.

Still, you need to expect there will be skepticism for a long, long time. These people have heard promises before, and those promises were not fulfilled. So, while it's critical to start making changes right away, it's also important not to over-promise on things you may not be able to deliver. Make modest, achievable, positive changes, and then build from there.

Some of the changes you make may involve implementing policies that require new behaviors. Some may call for belt-tightening or restricting access to resources and capital. When you need to make such potentially unpopular changes, communication is critical. The better you can explain the reasons for the changes to the people affected by them, the better your chances of achieving buy-in. Particularly for big policy changes, it's wise to have town-hall meetings, in which the planned change is discussed in a transparent way, and everyone has an opportunity to ask questions and offer suggestions. Sit down with every influential leader in the organization that you can, get their perspective, and explain why the change needs to happen. In these conversations, of course, always be open to suggestions that may improve your plan.

Change only a few things at a time

After you assume your leadership position and do your initial analyses, you may realize there are thirty-four major things that need to change in the organization. Don't make the mistake of trying to change everything at once. When it comes to consequential changes, focus on a manageable number, which will vary based on the distribution of impact of the changes and the level of effort needed to implement each. Change is difficult, and people have limited time and ability to focus. If you overwhelm them with too many demands, you'll fail at everything.

I once served in an organization where the senior leadership issued a list of eighty-five top priorities it expected teams to implement. This is ridiculous on multiple levels. No one can juggle eighty-five priorities. And so, what happens (as it did in this organization) is that every department looks at the list and realizes that, at best, it can achieve six to ten of the priorities within the next year or two. Each of the subordinate organizations then makes its own decision about which goals to tackle and when. Senior leadership thus abdicates its responsibility and dilutes its authority, allowing the "chickens to run the henhouse." There is no alignment across the organization; everybody's rowing in separate directions.

Far better to get full alignment on a few things than to have misalignment on many.

Try to restore the joy in practicing medicine

Physician burnout is a big topic in medical literature these days. What's probably being expressed by many doctors, even if not actual burnout, is a sense of frustration and annoyance. The bureaucratic requirements of our jobs—increased reporting and record-keeping, insurance hoops to jump through, EMR management, etc.—are detracting in an odious way from our primary mission: taking care of patients. We didn't become doctors because we wanted to do paperwork. We became doctors because we wanted to care for patients.

Part of your role as a physician leader, then, is to bring a doctor's perspective to the table and make sure your organization's policies are not creating *unnecessary* bureaucratic burdens. You should also do everything in your power to lessen the burdens doctors are already facing. As you probably know, physicians in your organization are swamped with licensing requirements, continuing education requirements, government requirements, organizational requirements, and more. Doing required dictation and documentation subtracts from the time they can spend caring for patients. Reports in some specialties show that for every hour of patient contact, doctors are doing three hours of EMR work. If that's even fractionally true, it's a massive burden. And so, you should advocate for physicians, nurses, and patients by doing whatever you can to streamline, reduce, or eliminate non-value-added work.

> *When doctors and nurses are happy in their practice, both staff and patients benefit.*

A noble goal for a physician leader is to try to restore the joy in medicine. When doctors and nurses are happy in their practice, both staff and patients benefit. One thing leaders can do, at a bare minimum, is to provide offsets whenever adding a new requirement to the job. In other words, if you're asking people to do an added step that will take fifteen minutes every day, what are you willing to take away? Doctors' and nurses' schedules are already overly full. If a new requirement is really important, then which of the fifty-seven old requirements will you delete so they have time to do it? If you can pare back the paperwork so that doctors can spend five additional minutes with each patient every day, you will be a hero to doctors, and you will gain many allies in the physicians' ranks.

Stepping into an organizational leadership position will always feel uncomfortable. You're playing a new role and have many new things to learn. But it shouldn't feel wholly unnatural, and it shouldn't create turmoil or setbacks in the organization. If you have been thinking about leadership for years and refining your leadership skills, then the step to organizational leadership should feel like an incremental change, not like landing on a new planet. It's not so different from learning surgery—you start with smaller, simpler cases and build to more complicated ones.

Just as we would never drop a new surgeon-in-training into a very complicated surgical case, we shouldn't be dropping physicians with no leadership training into complex senior leadership roles. We should, and we can, do a better job of preparing them along the way. We've been talking about this throughout the book. In the next section, we'll look at some specific ways we can improve leadership training throughout physicians' careers.

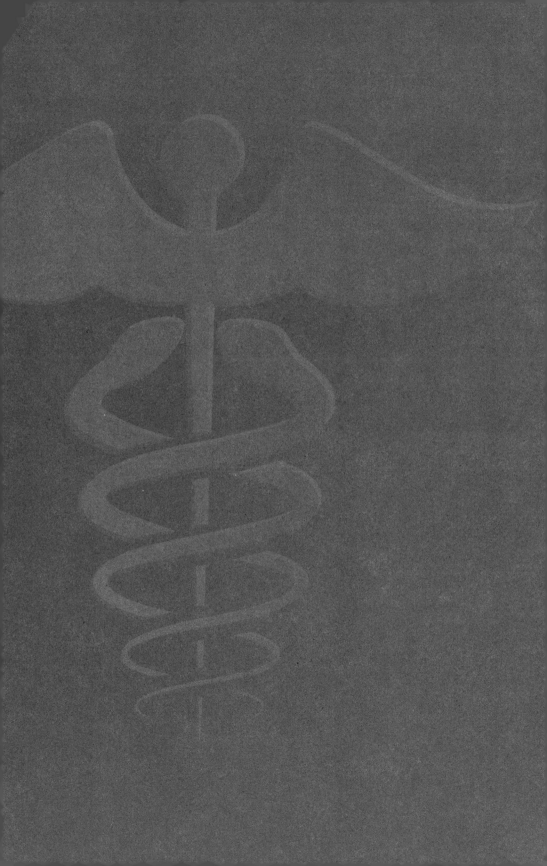

Redefining Physician Leadership at the Institutional Level

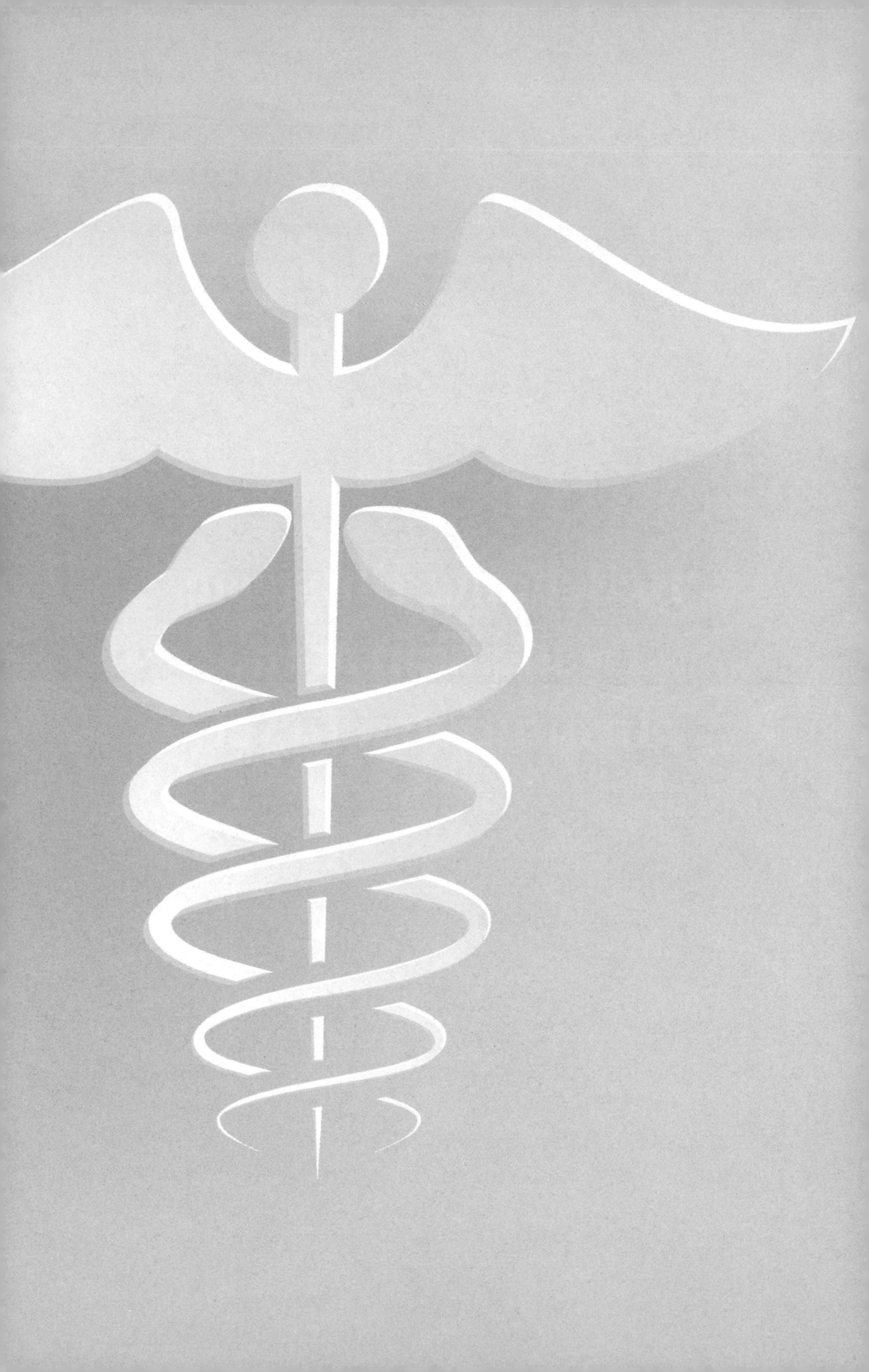

CHAPTER 8

The Four Essential Lines of Effort (LOEs)

The most dangerous leadership myth is that leaders are born—that there is a genetic factor to leadership… in fact, the opposite is true. Leaders are made rather than born.

- WARREN BENNIS

Section 1 of this book was about the Why—the reasons it's important to incorporate leadership training into the education and career of practicing physicians from day one. Physicians are already de facto leaders in the eyes of their patients, their team members, their residents, and the community at large. By failing to train them fully and formally as such, we leave their leadership development to chance and weaken their ability to *influence thought and behavior to achieve desired results*. Thus, we fail to optimize patient care. We can and should do better.

Section 2 dealt mainly with the How—a conceptual framework for training leaders that starts with Leading Yourself and then proceeds outward to Leading Another, Leading Teams, and Leading Organizations. We looked at some of the skillsets needed to excel at each of these levels and some of the challenges to be faced.

Here in Section 3, we'll concern ourselves chiefly with the What—what kinds of programs and changes we can implement in medical schools and residencies, healthcare systems, and professional societies to better prepare physicians for the leadership challenges they already are facing. Whereas the first two sections are of greatest interest to physicians, this section is meant to include the people responsible for implementing the leadership training ideas we'll be discussing. Of course, physicians will be interested in this material too, as will other healthcare professionals.

This section will be considerably shorter than the previous sections. I won't present pages upon pages of eye-glazing details about specific curriculum choices—courses, books, programs, training sessions, etc.—but rather will offer some general ways to think about building leadership training into a physician's career. Each institution will have its own way of handling the details, its own goals and values, and its own specific curricula.

As an overall framework for training physician leadership, however, I would like to suggest a four-pronged approach that emerged from the work my coauthors and I did in creating the framework of the physician leadership development program for the 4,200 doctors in the US Army.

The Four LOEs

I've been referring to the military since page one of the book. That's not only because I received my own leadership training in the military but also because the US Armed Forces are nothing short of leadership factories. They are designed from top to bottom for the purpose of training leaders. And it's easy to understand why. It's the nature of the military that leaders often need to assume a new leadership position on a moment's notice and that people constantly move through the ranks. The military knows it can't afford to wait until leaders step into their designated roles before starting their training. Leadership-thinking must be engrained from day one. There must be a ready "bench" of trained leaders waiting to be called up when their time arrives. For that reason, the military has put more thought and execution into leadership training than any other organization. They know what works and what doesn't.

> *The military knows it can't afford to wait until leaders step into their designated roles before starting their training.*

When creating the US Army Medical Corps' physician leadership program, our design group formed the guiding opinion that "junior Medical Corps officers [should] receive programmatic, ongoing leadership education throughout medical school, residency and early in their careers with practical opportunities to observe and actively participate in activities designed to foster leadership development."[20] We further concluded, "These skills and training should be provided in small increments over an entire career rather than in large increments followed by periods where the skills are not exercised."[21]

We identified four main LOEs (lines of effort) through which the above could be accomplished. The US Army Doctrine Publication (ADP) 3-0 defines an LOE as "a line that links multiple tasks using the logic of purpose… to focus efforts toward establishing a desired end state. Lines of effort are essential to long-term planning."[22]

For each LOE, we also looked at how things were handled in outside organizations such as the Veterans Health Administration and civilian healthcare systems and associations. All ideas were encouraged, and divergent opinions and ideas were welcomed. Robust discussions took place.

The four LOEs we recommended—taken verbatim from the report we delivered[23]—were:

1. Develop Interest—*early exposure to leadership theory and practice*

2. The Foundation—*provide leadership education*

3. Apprenticeship Refined—*mentorship and coaching*

4. Building the Bench—*identify, recruit, and build experience for future senior leaders*

---

20   "All Physicians Lead." The U.S. Army Medical Corps Leadership Development Program (2012). Editors Colonel Lean E. Moores & Colonel Chuck Callahan. p. 11.

21   Ibid., p. 11.

22   Army Publishing Directorate, The US Army Doctrine Publication 3-0, accessed September 15, 2023, https://armypubs.army.mil/epubs/DR_pubs/DR_a/ARN18010-ADP_3-0-000-WEB-2.pdf.

23   Moores and Callahan, op. cit., p. 11.

We'll look at each in more detail below.

Given how much work and study is already required of young physicians, we decided that implementation of these LOEs "must minimize any additional administrative and resource burdens at all levels."[24] In other words, we did not want to add a whole new layer of burdensome requirements and time commitments for physicians-in-training or their trainers. To the degree possible, we felt leadership development should dovetail with trainings and structures already in place.

As we were identifying these LOEs, it quickly became clear to us that this four-pronged approach would work equally well with nonmilitary doctors. The structures for implementing the LOEs would be different in the civilian world, but the LOEs would be essentially the same.

Develop interest (early exposure to leadership theory and practice)

The very first requirement for developing leadership in physicians is to pique their interest, early in their careers, in the idea that leadership—that is, the ability to *influence thought and behavior to achieve desired results*—is critical to the work they do. As noted earlier, doctors-in-training tend to be a bit dismissive of courses that teach "soft skills"—not necessarily because they view this type of work as unimportant but because they're forced to exercise a sort of "intellectual triage." There is only so much time in each day or week, and student doctors have more important things to do, such as learning anatomy and pharmacology. Anything that detracts from the time spent acquiring clinical skills and knowledge is placed, almost by necessity, on the back burner.

What if, however, from the first day of their education, physicians could learn to see leadership as *integral* to the work they do with patients

---

24   Ibid. p. 8.

and teammates, rather than a distraction *from* it? They would likely be more inclined to embrace their leadership development as time went on.

There are two important ways we should look at developing leadership interest in young physicians. The first is by helping them see leadership as an essential part of clinical practice: doctors lead patients, doctors lead coworkers, doctors lead teams. We have been talking about this kind of leadership throughout the book. Senior physicians should train young doctors in leadership skills simultaneously with their teaching of clinical skills—for example, by praising the way they readied a trauma bay team for a procedure in addition to the way they performed the procedure. In this way, young doctors would come to see leadership as part of their job.

The second essential way to develop interest is to help them see their role as part of an overall system. As soon as a new physician hits the ground, we should get them involved in some aspect of hospital business. There are dozens of committees that need help, and there are never enough people to run them. Some of these committees may lack physician voices. This is a perfect opportunity for a young physician to make an organizational contribution right away. By serving on a committee, the young doctor brings a fresh perspective to the table while simultaneously absorbing the wisdom and experience of the senior people in the room. Many critical decisions are made away from the bedside, and it can be helpful to have physicians' voices in the rooms where these decisions are being made.

Committee membership could be treated almost like an internship for young physicians. Thus, the physician would learn, early on, that running a healthcare system is complicated, that resources are limited, and other such truths. He or she would get to see how other professionals in the organization think and begin to appreciate the degree of nonclinical expertise that's required to keep a hospital running. This kind of exposure is essential as we develop the next generation of organizational leaders.

Serving on committees may also provide some of the first real insight physicians gain into group dynamics—how to put together an agenda, how to draw out the opinion of someone who may not be participating fully, how to deal with a person who constantly tries to hijack the meeting, and so on.

The foundation (provide leadership education)

A solid leadership education is the foundation upon which a career's worth of leadership development is built. This leadership education should be provided as part of medical school training, which we will discuss briefly in the next chapter, and should continue thereafter via healthcare organizations and physicians' societies.

Ideally, there should be an element of standardization in leadership training—a core curriculum—just as there is in a doctor's clinical training, while also allowing room for each medical school to provide its own perspectives and focus based upon its mission, vision, and values. In that way, healthcare organizations could be confident that all new hires would possess a base-level education in leadership theory and practice. This core curriculum could also be used as a touchstone for catch-up and review throughout a physician's career.

It is important to emphasize that the tools and materials for providing leadership education for physicians are not new, and most are not specific to medicine. A wealth of great leadership literature already exists, and much of it is applicable to any profession. We don't need to reinvent the wheel when it comes to leadership theory and practice. Education providers can choose from existing training programs, books, and courses that fit best in their institution and tailor them to their specific needs.

Apprenticeship refined (mentorship and coaching)

The next important LOE is to develop a system of mentors, coaches, and other leaders who can work with physicians throughout their careers to develop their leadership abilities. The idea of mentorship and coaching is not new for doctors. Historically, medicine has always been a guild-like practice with an apprenticeship style of training. Younger physicians train alongside more experienced clinicians until they are deemed ready to practice on their own. But, as I've stated before, excellent teaching in clinical skills does not provide the skills that transfer to leadership development.

Medicine can use the supervisory and teaching structures already in place to develop leadership alongside clinical skills. We can also provide additional person-to-person leadership relationships to help. Specifically, *mentoring* and *coaching* can provide a leadership focus that may be absent from most physicians' ongoing training.

It is helpful to be clear about our terminology here. Consistency in the usage of terms like coaching and mentoring allows us and our learners to be clear about some of the nuance that each role provides and sets appropriate expectations. Coaching and mentoring have different focuses, the terms are often confused, and both differ from the type of guidance typically given by bosses and senior clinicians. Both coaching and mentoring are important as we make leadership development a central focus in physicians' careers.

Coaching tends to be short term and focused on developing specific skills that directly affect various aspects of job performance. A coach, for example, might work with a doctor on their cultural competency skills or their listening skills.

Mentorship, by contrast, is a longer-term relationship that looks at a person's overall career and the opportunities and challenges that present themselves along the way. Mentorship is usually provided by a senior individual with seasoned experience. This person may be outside the organization, or at least outside the "chain of command," so the mentee can speak freely about any challenges they may be facing in their current position. Mentors should be sounding boards as well as guides. A boss, for that reason, has limited potential as a mentor. A leadership mentor who focuses on the physician's personal development, not just their clinical skills, is a vital player.

Coaching can be effectively used in medicine to help patch gaps in physicians' leadership skillsets and to help prepare physicians for specific leadership roles. Mentoring can and should play a valuable role in leadership development across the entire physician career spectrum.

Every new doctor also has bosses such as teaching faculty, senior residents, and fellows. These individuals often provide some coaching- and mentorship-like guidance, but their main focus is making sure the physician is performing well in the clinical role for which he or she was hired and is functioning well within their teams. Still, leadership refinement should be part of their focus as well.

Another useful role is that of *sponsor*. In the military, when you transfer to a new unit, you're assigned a sponsor, and this person's job is to help you organize your life. Sponsors show you where the grocery store is and which neighborhoods to live in. They help get you settled in and serve as a local point of contact. Sponsorship can help cover some of the practical, day-to-day guidance so bosses, coaches, and mentors can play their roles more cleanly. Acting as a sponsor can also provide an "entry-level" way for young doctors to begin practicing their one-on-one leadership skills.

There is some overlap among all these roles, of course, but all should be recognized for their unique purposes and used in a deliberate, thoughtful way to help develop leadership.

Building the bench (identify, recruit, and build experience for future senior leaders)

Finally, we need to develop systems for identifying physicians with leadership potential and providing them with the experience and training they need to further develop their skills, with an eye toward eventual organizational leadership.

Healthcare has a tremendous need for leadership-ready physicians to fill roles within organizations.

Healthcare has a tremendous need for leadership-ready physicians to fill roles within organizations. The turnover rates in many of these positions are high, and extended gaps create operational challenges for healthcare organizations.

So, as we're working on LOEs 1–3, above, we're also looking to identify potential leaders to be part of a succession pipeline—our "bench." Toward this end, there should be people within our organizations specifically tasked with looking at physicians serving on committees and evaluating their leadership potential and their training needs. Whenever we offer educational courses, we should have senior leaders in the courses alongside the junior leaders acting as "talent scouts," observing them and providing feedback to the organization. Mentors and coaches should be doing the same. The idea is to identify "superstars" with leadership potential as early as possible, to find out where their training gaps are, and then to provide these promising individuals with the education and experience they need to grow their abilities.

We should also be looking at factors such as the temperaments and leadership styles of these junior leaders we're identifying. Who are the commanding and pacesetting types and who are the more democratic and affiliative types, and where would they best serve, respectively?

This kind of information will become available to us as we learn to perform the first three LOEs thoughtfully and attentively.

These four LOEs should form our multipronged approach to training physicians as leaders, both in their current role as practicing doctors and for future promotion within organizations. This will involve coordinated work among educational institutions, healthcare systems, and professional societies for physicians, which we'll look at in the next chapter.

CHAPTER 9

Schools, Systems, and Societies

Before you are a leader,
success is all about growing yourself.
After you become a leader,
success is all about growing others.

- JACK WELCH

In this final chapter, we will look at some ways leadership training can be implemented and improved throughout physicians' careers. The three entities that will play the largest roles in revamping the way we train doctors as leaders are physician training institutes (schools of medicine and graduate medical education (GME) programs—residencies and fellowships), healthcare systems and organizations, and physicians' professional societies such as the American College of Surgeons and the American College of Physicians.

Before we talk about how each of these three entities can help, let's talk about an overall guiding vision, as well as the current reality we're facing.

Vision and Present Reality

It is my belief—as I've been preaching throughout the book—that we should be teaching leadership as a core competency for all physicians. It should be presented as foundational, much in the same way we teach physiology and pharmacology and how to tie a surgical knot. These latter skills form the bricks upon which medical careers are built. I want us to recognize that *influencing thought and behavior to achieve desired results* is an equally integral part of what physicians do—numerous times every day—and we should build a solid foundation in how to accomplish that. A physician who is a less effective leader is a less effective doctor.

> *If you don't start thinking about leadership until you're fifty, you've lost a huge opportunity to gain that mastery.*

Malcolm Gladwell famously pointed out that 10,000 hours of practice is required to achieve mastery in a skill area. It stands to reason that if you don't start thinking about leadership until you're fifty, you've lost a huge opportunity to gain that mastery. True, you may have been practicing various *aspects* of leadership for decades, but if you don't recognize it as such and reflect on it consciously, you miss an opportunity to refine and augment your skills. Conversely, if you've been actively thinking about leadership and working on it for the first twenty years of your career you'll be at a much more advanced stage by age fifty.

In 1910, the Flexner Report changed medicine forever by identifying gaps and inconsistencies in medical education and recommending sweeping changes in the standards for medical schools. My personal vision is that we will develop a similar set of standards for the leadership aspects of a physician's training. Eventually, this set of standards would be adopted and refined by the various oversight bodies that guide physicians' careers, such as the Liaison Committee on Medical Education (LCME), the American Council on Graduate Medical Education (ACGME), and the American Board of Medical Specialties (ABMS). These bodies have prescriptive authority. They can say to medical schools and healthcare organizations, "This is what you need to be teaching and practicing," and can work with these entities, over time, to ensure that all doctors have a common training in a fundamental leadership skillset.

Standardization would benefit healthcare system leaders, as they would know that newly hired doctors possess a base level of leadership competency, much as they now know that all doctors possess a base level of clinical competency. Every physician will have been thinking about leadership, doing self-assessments, undergoing 360-degree assessments, and refining his or her leadership skills for years.

The organization can then build on that base set of competencies to further develop the physician leader.

That is the vision. But let me quickly add that we are a long way from seeing that as a reality. I have no illusions that such a change will happen overnight. The medical establishment changes slowly. Incorporating structured leadership training into every medical school and healthcare system can take decades.

That said, the implementation should aim at codifying a set of base-level skills that can be generally agreed upon as a good leadership foundation for all doctors.

In the meantime, let's advance the conversation. (I hope this book helps.) Let's start addressing topics such as "All Physicians Lead" at conferences and symposia. Let's get to work within our own organizations to develop in-house standards for physician leadership. Let's start creating leadership curricula and sharing it with other institutions and organizations. Let's start developing courses (see next sections), implementing them, and measuring results. Let's start assigning leadership coaches and mentors to doctors in our system.

The curricula we develop should cover important skills in each of the four concentric circles of leadership—whether we use that terminology and framework or not. Doctors should be trained in how to lead themselves, other individuals, and teams. Those who show potential should be further trained in organizational leadership.

For a while, we'll have to do "needs assessments" of every new doctor and resident who enters our system, to see where they stand in relation to our in-house standards. If they've had good training in the past, we can start them at "300-level" course material, but if they've had virtually no leadership training, we'll need to start them at 101. The basic formula we can use is (1) develop a set of leadership competency expectations, (2) assess where the gaps are, both within our system and within individuals entering our system, and (3) create trainings to close the gaps.

Over time, as more of us do this work, a functional set of standards will evolve, which, ideally, will later form the basis of a codified set of standards and curricula. This too will undergo change and refinement as organizations learn what works and what doesn't.

Physician Training Institutions

Medical schools can lead the way in establishing the conviction in young physicians that they are leaders and igniting the desire to be trained as such. By linking leadership skills to the improved performance of healthcare teams and better patient outcomes, schools can change the current culture in which student doctors relegate "soft skills" to the back burner as they focus on clinical training. Again, this will not be an easy task.

A joke I've heard springs to mind:

> *How many medical school faculty does it take to change a light bulb?*
>
> *Hard to say. First you need to get past the look of horror on everyone's faces as they exclaim, "CHANGE? No one told us there was going to be CHANGE!"*

All kidding aside, injecting new content into a medical school's curriculum is a time-consuming process. It can take years of debate to change a twenty-minute section of a biochemistry course. Anyone who thinks they're going to steal ten hours of contact time away from, say, anatomy, to teach leadership is in for a dog fight. Realistically, we can't take hours of instruction away from core clinical courses. Nor would we want to. So, the trick is to find places in the curriculum where we're already teaching "leadership-like" topics and to organize and revamp that material in a more cohesive and powerful way.

For example, a school may offer courses on communication skills, cultural competency, organizational skills, and other similar topics but may not be labeling them as leadership courses. We can identify all this disparate training, remove redundancies, fill in gaps, optimize it, and pull it together under the banner of leadership. Then we can teach it with a four-year growth perspective in mind. So, instead of scattering "leadership 101" topics throughout the four years, we would teach foundational courses in the first year. In the second and third years we can offer progressively advanced topics on how to influence thought and behavior. In the fourth year we might offer a capstone project in which students are placed in simulated scenarios that present difficult challenges from both a leadership and a clinical perspective.

Again, the concentric circles of leadership can serve as a good basis for organizing the learning materials, but individual schools may have their own organizational approaches.

Once medical schools are doing this, residency training programs and physician employers can build from there. The leadership curriculum should never end. Everyone in medicine should ideally continue to seek and receive leadership training and feedback throughout their careers. (This is similar to our training for military leaders; even generals and admirals attend leadership development courses to hone their skills.) Medical schools will play a big role in getting the ball rolling.

An early model

I'm proud to report that my alma mater, The Uniformed Services University of the Health Sciences (USU) School of Medicine in Bethesda, Maryland, has been among the first schools to recognize the need for an ascending progression of leadership education spanning four years of medical school for all students. It has revamped its curriculum to embed leadership training in doctors' education in a four-year, progressive manner, much as I've been prescribing in this book. USU recently graduated its first class of physicians trained this way.

The following description of USU's curriculum is taken directly from an article in *Military Medicine* called "Leadership Education and Development at the Uniformed Services University":

> The curriculum is built on core attributes of effective and ethical leadership and officership, including:
>
> - Knowledge of self
>
> - Adherence to core values
>
> - Personal mission and vision
>
> - Adherence to fundamental military standards and behaviors
>
> - Physical, mental, and emotional fitness
>
> - Effective followership
>
> - Communication skills
>
> - Conflict resolution
>
> - Teamwork and teambuilding
>
> - Problem-solving and decision-making
>
> - Planning and organization
>
> - Mission focus
>
> - Technical competence
>
> - Resource stewardship
>
> - Risk analysis and focus on safety

- Development and welfare of subordinates

- Relationship with the line, the American public, and its elected representatives

Our curriculum is also based on the idea that for career military medical officers to progress as an officer and leader, they must first master the basic knowledge, skills, and attitudes required of a junior medical officer right out of medical school. Over time, a capable officer can build on these core attributes and develop the necessary skills to hold a senior staff position or even command a large military medical organization. To accomplish these goals, students must develop and function on a continuum that starts with leading oneself at the individual level and ends with leading others in large, complex organizations.[25]

Does that sound familiar? The article goes on to point out:

Although this curriculum is oriented to the military medical officer in an operational setting, the knowledge, skills, and attitudes are highly applicable to the more conventional clinical environment and will serve to reinforce the leadership, officership, and professionalism required in the practice of clinical medicine.[26]

In other words, though a few of USU's course elements are specific to the military, most are applicable in any medical school or healthcare system.

---

25 Francis G. O'Connor, Neil Grunberg, Arthur L. Kellermann, and Eric Schoomaker, "Leadership Education and Development at the Uniformed Services University," *Military Medicine* 180, no. 4: 147, 149.

26 Ibid., p. 149.

Healthcare Systems and Hospitals

Healthcare organizations can and should reinforce, refine, and advance the leadership training that begins in medical school. They can do this both through the residency and fellowship programs they host and through the ongoing training opportunities they provide for staff physicians.

Residencies and Fellowships

Residencies and fellowships, as the next step in a physician's training, should build directly on the leadership skills young physicians begin to learn in medical school. Working with the ACGME and residency designated institutional officials, or DIOs (the hospital's physician leader who has authority for oversight of the residency programs), healthcare systems can bring leadership training to our most junior physicians.

When new physicians enter postgraduate residency training, they begin receiving feedback from residency program directors and faculty in the hospital rather than the medical school. There are now numerous other professionals to their left and right in many healthcare disciplines. Ideally, these professionals would be talking to each resident and observing their leadership development. Again, the concentric circles model can provide the framework for this (mainly the first three circles; organizational leadership can come later). Does the resident have good self-confidence and self-awareness? How is he or she doing leading patients and other team members on a one-on-one basis? And of course, how is the resident's team leadership? The ability to lead high-performing teams should receive a great deal of focus at the residency level, because, having just now put on the long white coat of a doctor instead of the short white coat of a medical student, this is typically the young doctor's first real immersion in team leadership.

Residency is a great place to focus on the specific educational needs of the individual learner. We already do this on the clinical level. If we see a resident struggling, for example, with a particular technique in the operating room, we take them aside to coach them on the nuances of that skill. Leadership training should be no different. If we observe a resident having a difficult interaction with a team member, for example, we might say, "Let's do some work on managing conflict." And then we might give them a book about that topic and assign them a couple of chapters to read and discuss the following week. Or we might send them to a course on conflict management.

Part of the challenge, as we develop this new culture, will be inconsistency among medical schools. Some will be graduating people with a thorough grounding in leadership skills, others won't. When we start building a leadership curriculum within a residency program, we'll have to do a needs assessment to figure out where our learners are. First-year residents will likely have varying levels of leadership training and experience. So, we may need to offer a catch-up curriculum, much in the way we teach remedial skills to incoming college students who are lagging in writing or math.

Staff physicians

When it comes to leadership, healthcare organizations have multiple levels of need. First, they want their staff of physicians to be leading their colleagues, teams, and patients effectively, for all the reasons we've been discussing throughout the book. But they also want to build a leadership pipeline at the organizational level.

The system, again, must start by clarifying its needs and standards. What do we want from our doctors, leadership-wise? What are our organizational values? Our goals? What do we want our physician leaders to look like and act like?

Then the organization must look at how it's getting there. What kind of performance evaluation are we using for our physician leaders? What training are we providing? Is it sufficient? Are there gaps in our evaluation, our training, our measurement methods? Some organizations have a fantastic system for evaluating leaders but provide no training whatsoever. Others provide a lot of training but have no outcome measures. It's vital to have clear leadership goals, good evaluation methods, great training, and meaningful ways to measure what's working and what isn't.

A healthcare system has the ability to offer comprehensive long-term training because it "owns" its physicians' time while they're affiliated with the system. So, there are opportunities to give doctors protected time for study and also devise a curriculum that will hold their attention for a full year—or three years or five years.

It is unreasonable to think any system can spend tens of thousands of dollars on every one of its new doctor positions, but it can do some general training for everyone. It might offer, for example, a web-based learning program, or it might incorporate leadership training into grand rounds. Another idea might be to host an annual leadership day, much in the same way that some systems host research days. Speakers and courses on physician leadership could be available all day long, and this event could become a highly anticipated, integral part of organizational culture. And when physicians show promise and interest in any of the above "entry-level" trainings, they could be provided with more tailored and advanced opportunities.

A large healthcare organization might need to offer multiple tiers of training—for example, one tier for all physicians, another tier for mid-career doctors to prepare them for senior roles, and yet another tier for senior physicians already in leadership positions. Within each tier, it would still need to assess each individual's knowledge gaps and measure their progress. It's a big task, but the payoff is enormous for the present and future health of the organization. By providing this type of education and training, healthcare systems would incentivize many physicians to stay in the organization. This will prove to be a great asset when looking toward developing a leadership pipeline. Additionally, from a financial ROI lens, since the cost of a single physician turnover can reportedly run from $250,000 to $1,000,000, a small improvement in retention can pay for some, if not all, of a physician leadership development program. You can build loyalty by *showing you care* through investment in the physicians' development.

The leadership pipeline

Building the bench is another area where healthcare organizations must do thorough needs assessments. What are our leadership needs? How many leadership positions do we have to fill? In a large healthcare system, for example, we might need as many as five to ten physician leaders in the C-suite, thirty to fifty at the hospital leadership level, and fifty to hundred at the department level. That's a lot of leaders. And turnover is an issue; we might be losing thirty physician leaders a year. How are we replacing them, and how thoughtful are we being? How well trained are the folks we're moving into these positions? What is our current methodology for getting people ready for those leadership roles? How do we assess their performance in those roles?

A program example

Let's consider a hypothetical healthcare system. "Shore Health System" leadership is concerned that too many doctors are being promoted to leadership positions without sufficient training, and it is interested in improving the effectiveness of its entire physician staff and to better train them for both current responsibilities and future leadership positions. And so, the CEO decides to create a multitiered, in-house "leadership development academy," with the goals (among others) of improving the leadership education of all physicians. By doing so, it also hopes to develop a pipeline of trusted, culture-changing leaders for the future.

Early recommendations for creating the program are:

- Appoint and convene a Physician Leadership Development Committee—to develop a charter and delineate resource requirements.

- Establish a Director of Physician Leadership.

- Define the method by which physicians will be chosen to participate in the structured Leadership Program.

- Research and select leadership development assessment tools.

Some features of its proposed physician leadership academy are:

- Whenever possible, use in-house leaders as faculty to increase partnerships. Almost all systems have MBA, MHA, doctorate, or military-experienced leaders who can pitch in here.

- Establish a formal onboarding program for all physicians.

- Develop a mentor training program. (As with leadership, mentorship can be taught!)

- Create a three-tiered program:

  1. Develop a core leadership curriculum for all physicians (seminars, webinars, speaker's bureau, online content, reading lists, podcasts, etc.). Start a mentoring program for all new physicians.

2. Develop a structured leadership development program for current and future leaders. This would entail specific coursework as well as mentorship and coaching for current leaders in defined positions.

3. Identify potential future C-suite level leaders and provide higher-level education and training. Support certificate and advanced degree programs with some form of cost-sharing between the physician and the system.

- Create a curriculum to include such topics as:

  □ *Personal development as a leader*

  - Assessing self-awareness

  - Leadership styles

  - Caring, communication, and consistency—the "Triad of Effective Leadership"

  □ *Managing people and relationships*

  - Performance management

  - Power, influence, and authority

  - Managing conflict

  - Negotiation

  - Recruiting and developing talent, mentoring

  - Team dynamics

  - Difficult conversations

  - Legal landmines in human resource management

    ◻ *Managing groups and projects*

- Project planning and management

- Organizational alignment

- Change management

- Meeting management

- Managing teams

    ◻ *Managerial finance and accounting*

- Financial statements, funds accounting

- Revenue cycles, cost accounting, budgets

- Incentives

- Business plans

    ◻ *Understanding the system*

- Organizational structure—hospital, healthcare system

- Planning and decision matrix development

- Finances

- Decision-makers in the organization

- Create an annual leadership day for physicians and physicians-in-training.

- Develop a comprehensive tool for tracking leadership development and ROI of the leadership program. This could include:

    ◻ Initial assessment, using 360-degree feedback from supervisors, peers, and direct reports; questionnaires; Myers–

Briggs Type Indicator; Thomas–Kilmann Conflict Mode Instrument, and others.

▫ Ongoing evaluation across a wide range of skills and capabilities, before and after training, such as ability to coach and give guidance, resolve conflicts, lead and support teams in meeting their objectives, etc.

▫ Goal setting and tracking

▫ Measuring and tracking financial ROI

The above is just a skeletal framework, but it suggests the kind of thinking that goes into developing a leadership program at the healthcare system level. A mixture of *types* of learning materials is ideal: reading assignments, courses, retreats, online "homework," case studies, mentoring, coaching, role-playing sessions, and individualized leadership plans.

Professional Societies

Professional associations are another excellent resource to both make the case for better leadership training for physicians and provide some of that training and education.

Medical societies have existed for hundreds of years and some US medical societies have charters going back more than a century. These associations are typically formed for the purpose of helping members with career development, networking, research, continuing education, and improving standards of practice. There are the American College of Surgeons (ACS), American College of Cardiology, American College of Radiology, American Academy of Dermatology, etc. Every medical specialty has a professional society that does similar things, tailored to their members' specific needs.

These societies create bylaws, appoint boards of directors and CEOs or presidents, and often develop clinical, behavioral, and educational standards for their members. Over time, they become influential. They hold sway with their members and with the medical world at large. Some of them also have separate political action committees.

Membership in physicians' societies has benefits. If you've been a member in good standing of, for example, the ACS for a certain number of years and have a strong clinical and citizenship record, you can be voted to become a fellow. And those letters, FACS (Fellow of the American College of Surgeons), after your MD have meaning and substance in the medical world.

These professional societies often gather annually or semi-annually at large venues. The conventions can be quite large, with over ten thousand members attending. The purposes of the gatherings may include governance, education, networking, familiarization with updated equipment and techniques, job postings, and mentorship. Numerous small seminars and discussion groups are offered, as well as large keynote addresses. Members also meet to talk about important issues and concerns, such as how members are obtaining access to training for a new diagnostic tool. Recommendations and action plans emerge. A major focus of these events is to propagate change throughout the professional cohort.

Ideas presented at annual gatherings have tremendous reach, because thousands of specialized doctors are gathered under the same roof for the expressed purpose of learning. These events offer a fantastic opportunity to provide leadership education and training for physicians and to talk to physicians about how to develop leadership within their own organizations.

On the other hand, Such venues are limited in their ability to provide sustained, focused coursework over a long period, the way a school or a healthcare organization can. Members of professional societies are geographically dispersed and represent a heterogeneous mix of leadership, experience, education, and training. Because of this, there are fewer opportunities for consecutive contact hours than in a healthcare system. The type of training that associations can typically offer is concentrated packages of information tailored to be given out over perhaps a two-, three-, or five-year period. (This may be changing, now that Zoom and other online meeting technologies have become widely accepted.)

My hope and recommendation is that physician societies and associations take up the banner of physician leadership as a major focus in the coming years. At annual meetings, they can offer provocative lectures and discussions on leadership topics that expand upon the training doctors receive in schools and healthcare organizations. They can also drill down into specific leadership-related issues such as measuring educational ROI and the importance of physician leadership in a value-based reimbursement environment.

Given the brief and annual contact with the majority of members, perhaps the best value societies can provide is a longitudinal assessment program taken by members (similar to an annual physical) that can track and trend important performance measures.

A sampling of other topics that might be explored through association events:

- Strategic decision-making and good patient care

- Raising patient satisfaction scores through improved leadership

- Leading up

- Overcoming cognitive biases as a leader

- Psychological safety as a key to high team performance

- Higher staff engagement = better patient outcomes

- Hidden traps in cultural competency efforts

- The art of framing choices for patients

- Funding and payment mechanisms

- Managing cultural conflicts

- Addressing bad behavior

- How to align clinical initiatives with organizational goals

- Leading change

- Funding and payment mechanisms

- Recruiting for cultural fit versus recruiting for cultural *change*

- Creating a leadership mentoring program for physicians

There are hundreds more topics that could be presented.

A side benefit

One reason doctors' associations should be interested in building leaders is that they, too, have a need for leaders within their societies. Groups typically have a society president, a first vice president, a secretary, and so on. There are also program committee chairs, people who run the educational programs, people who are involved in the foundation, and more. Societies, therefore, have good reason to pay attention to the leadership development of the people in the organization.

Physicians' associations should do their own needs assessment in this regard. What are our organizational needs in terms of leadership? How many positions do we need to fill? What are our ongoing leadership needs? What are we doing now to meet those needs? How are we measuring our success? How do we get our future leaders ready for the positions they're going to hold, given the constraints of spread-out geography and limited contact hours?

Part of that assessment is to find out what their learners already know, and then provide them the tools to close any gaps.

Currently our professional societies put promising individuals on the leadership track just as healthcare organizations do. This model, which in many organizations seems to be reasonably effective, is to start leaders on a smaller committee, and then to increase responsibilities, making them vice chair, and then chair, and then move them to a bigger committee, etc. I submit we can do even better by adding structured leadership training—both general and individually tailored learning materials in a variety of formats.

Medical schools, healthcare organizations, and professional societies each have specific teaching opportunities based on contact hours, educational and experiential focus, and "ownership" of the learners' time. Schools can offer a thorough, four-year, graduated program in foundational leadership theory and practice. Healthcare organizations can augment this learning through hands-on teaching, coaching, and mentoring, as well as higher-level coursework and training on an ongoing basis. Physician associations can offer longitudinal assessment tools or shorter, more targeted learning opportunities that dig deeply into highly specific leadership topics and explore new angles of familiar topics that may be challenging or controversial. They can also, by virtue of their wide geographic reach, widely spread the message that physician leadership development is a vital need for the future of excellent medicine.

CLOSING UP

Thank you for reading this book. I hope I've at least *begun* to make my case to you: being a doctor means being a leader.

Follow any doctor throughout the course of her or his day—guiding a treatment team through morning rounds at the hospital, rallying the office staff for a day of patient appointments, meeting with individual patients, calling an insurance company to convince them to pay for a medication, initiating a phone consult with a colleague, calling patients at home to review test results and answer questions—and you will see a string of leadership events. People look to doctors to make excellent decisions and to guide them through life-changing and life-saving processes. That's what we do as physicians.

We are leaders, whether we recognize it or not. Our only real choice is whether to embrace our leadership role and commit to doing it to the very best of our ability. Or not.

Great physician leaders exude a presence. They bear themselves with confidence, but not cockiness. They look people in the eye. They listen to their patients, absorbing everything they're saying—and *not* saying. They treat colleagues warmly and respectfully. They speak with directness but also with compassion and sensitivity. They welcome questions, invite feedback, and are always trying to improve. They address doubts and uncertainties. They strive for consensus. When a good physician leader leaves the room, everyone feels uplifted and reassured, even if the medical situation is grave.

This kind of leadership presence has a direct bearing on the way patients commit to treatment and the way colleagues rally together as a team. Don't doubt for a second that it affects patient outcomes. It does.

If you are a physician, you should want to be the kind of leader who inspires people through your words, your actions, and your very presence. And if you are in healthcare management, you should want to have a staff full of physicians who possess this kind of leadership ability.

Fortunately, as I've been saying throughout this book, leadership is a learned skill. It starts with a thorough grounding in leadership theory and builds through practice, reflection, feedback, and coaching throughout each of the four concentric circles. Leaders are not born, they are made.

My hope is that every physician who reads this book makes a commitment to review their own leadership skillset and takes concrete steps toward filling any gaps. My even greater hope is that medical school deans, residency and fellowship program directors, healthcare administrators, and leaders of physicians' societies feel inspired to work together and take up the cause of teaching better leadership skills to physicians. In doing this, we will enrich the future of medicine, create higher performing healthcare teams, and improve patient outcomes.

For that, thank you very much.

If you would like to talk about
physician leadership development
in *your* organization, please visit:

AllPhysiciansLead.com

Dr. Leon Moores | *Healthcare Leadership Development Consultant*

Bringing with him over 30 years of medical leadership experience, including Chief of Surgery at Walter Reed Army Medical Center, CEO of Pediatric Specialists of Virginia, and president of the Inova Medical Group, Dr. Leon Moores is expanding his focus to encourage change across the medical profession.

Find out how Leon is getting the message out that all physicians are leaders, that leadership can be improved upon, and improved physician leadership in the clinic and at the bedside can result in better health outcomes for our patients.

ABOUT THE AUTHOR

LEON MOORES has studied and practiced leadership for over forty years in military and civilian settings. After graduating from West Point, he was commissioned an Infantry officer in the 82nd Airborne Division. He earned his MD from the Uniformed Services University (USU) School of Medicine and his Doctor of Science in Healthcare Leadership from the University of Alabama, Birmingham. Moores has served as Chief of Surgery at Walter Reed Army Medical Center, Deputy Commander (SVP) in National Naval Medical Center Bethesda, Commander (CEO) in Fort Meade Medical System, and CEO of Pediatric Specialists of Virginia. A practicing professor of pediatric neurosurgery, he most recently served as the CEO and president of the largest medical group in northern Virginia. He has earned the top leadership awards at West Point, the Army Infantry Officer Basic Course, the USU School of Medicine, and the War College, was twice named the Army Surgeon General's physician leader of the year, has been designated "Top Doctor" by *Washingtonian* and *Virginia* magazines, and has been awarded citations from the Governors of Maryland and Virginia. He is a sought-after speaker, author, and consultant in physician leadership.